NHL DRAFT GUIDE 2010

© 2010 by The Hockey Press
www.thehockeypress.com
All rights reserved.

ISBN # 0986538604
EAN-13 is 9780986538605.

Printed in the United States of America

HP Story

In 2004 I was coaching Wayne Simmonds in AAA hockey. It was crystal clear to me that Wayne had elite talent. I wondered how a player so talented could go under the radar and be completely missed by the hockey world. It was midway through that season that I had the idea, and HockeyProspect.com was born.

It's over 5 years later and Wayne has gone on to be a very good NHL player. I have been lucky enough to move along in the coaching ranks and have coached other players who are now in the NHL or will be very soon. HockeyProspect.com has taken monster steps forward since it's creation more than 5 years ago.. We have added more scouts and the websites traffic has grown to average over 29,000 unique visitors per month.

I'm most proud of the improvements in our team at HP. We have some truly talented scouts and equally talented writers and interviewers. We have some new ideas and hope that 2010/2011 will be even better.

Mark Edwards
Founder
HockeyProspect.com

Acknowledgements

This book would not have been possible without the efforts and long hours put in by our team of both scouts and writers. I'd like to especially thank Alex Linsky for his countless hours performing miracles out of my chicken scratch that I call scouting notes. I'd also like to thank Steve Fitzsimmons for his interview efforts both for this book and for our website over the last two seasons.

I'd also like to thanks E.J Maguire of NHL Central Scouting for taking the time to give us a few heights and weights we needed to verify.

Thanks guys.

Mark

Photo Credits

We want to thank Terry Wilson and Aaron Bell from OHL IMAGES for the use of their OHL, WHL and QMJHL player photos. Cover photos also from www.ohlimages.ca

We also want to thank David Arnold for his from the USHL and the Under 18 tournament in Belarus.
http://dga17.smugmug.com/

Maxim Kitsyn - Canada Hky Wikipedia

Nick Bjugstad - Howie Hanson StarTribune.com

Brock Nelson - Image used by permission from VintageMinnesotaHockey.com

Riley Sheahan - Matt Cashore mattcashore.com

Minnesota State Mavericks

WHL, OHL, QMJHL

Beau Bennett - Ryan Pinder
pentictonvees.podbean.com

Louis-Marc Aubry, Petr Straka Kirill Kabanov
Marc Grandmaison
www.marcgrandmaison.com

Contents

Part 1: Scouting Reports
Part 2: Player Interviews
Part 3: NHL Team Reports
Part 4: Player Rankings
Part 5: 2011 Draft Prospects

Preface

Taylor vs Tyler

It's something that NHL scouts and fans have been asking themselves all season long. If I had the first pick in the NHL Draft, who would I select? Would you take the battle hardened LW Taylor Hall of the Windsor Spitfires, who has won a Memorial Cup and was a key contributor at the World Juniors for Canada? Or would it be the slick pivot Seguin, who has found a way to make a silk purse out of a sow's ear on a less talented Plymouth team, who he's carried this season to greater heights than were expected? Another intriguing fact is that both players tied for the OHL Scoring title, albeit Hall in 5 less games.

With Taylor Hall you get a supremely talented player with world-class wheels. He is an elite skater who uses that to his best advantage and is a very aggressive forechecker, causing loads of problems for opposing players. He also has very soft hands and has shown he can be an elite scorer. He is also getting far better at finding line mates when he is covered. He can also dish the body and plays a physical brand of hockey. Just ask John Tavares.
During the playoffs last year, he ripped up the

OHL for 16 goals and 20 assists in 20 games. This year, he has already scored 6 goals and ten points in an opening round sweep of the Erie Otters. In three OHL seasons, he's shown steady progression from an impressive rookie season of 84 points to 90 points to 106 points. He also averaged two points a game at the World junior tournament for Canada and is clearly a winner.

As can be the case with high-level offensive players, he does need a little work on the defensive side of his game from a consistency standpoint. There is also the sentiment that he has the benefit of playing with elite players on the Memorial Cup champs. There is no denying the truth of that and the numbers back that up.

Windsor had 10 players with at least 43 points. Plymouth had 4 players with at least 43 points this campaign. That shows you the depth of the Spitfires attack, as compared to the Whalers offensively. Hall also had 3 first round NHL draft choices to play with on his club, while Seguin had none.

Tyler Seguin has a high compete level in all three zones and clearly takes pride in his defensive game. That did not stop him from posting 48 goals and 106 points in 63 games. As a playmaker, Seguin is one of the best in the draft class, having great vision to find his teammates through traffic and under coverage. He also skates well, but not in the elite level of Hall. He has been compared to a young Steve Yzerman and you can see why. Before the season people wondered if he was mostly a strong passer who wouldn't be a serious scorer, but Seguin answered that question with 48 goals this campaign.

While he didn't make Canada's world junior team like Hall did, that was not the end of the world for Seguin, who came back to the OHL very focused and had a massive run of points following that disappointment and took the league hostage on his offensive rampage. That for us shows a great deal of character.

We also like that he's posted the numbers he has with a much weaker supporting cast than Hall. Seguin was in on 43.2 percent of his team's goals this season, which was by far the highest percentage of any player in the OHL. Hall was on the score sheet for 32.0 percent of his club's goals.

Another interesting way of looking at the two players is to reverse the teams that each player played on. How would Seguin have performed in Windsor? How about Hall in Plymouth? That might give you another angle to think about.

But as far as who will go first overall, it probably comes down to an individual team's needs. Do they need a high level centre or an elite level winger? For HP.com, we think it's like a photo finish in a horse race, but at the wire we would select Tyler Seguin by a nose, but second overall this year is a lot like the 2008 Draft, with Steven Stamkos selected first and Drew Doughty taken second. No complaints will be coming from Los Angeles about their draft fate anytime soon.

1
SCOUTING REPORTS

Tyler Seguin

Center - Plymouth (OHL)
Born Jan 31 1992 Brampton, ONT
Height 6.01 Weight 186 Shoots R

SCOUTING REPORT

Tyler Seguin has come on strong and shot up the draft rankings since joining the Plymouth Whalers for the 2008-2009 season. He has become Taylor Hall's toughest competition for the #1 spot overall in this June's draft.

Seguin, a pure center, plays well in all three zones, and has shown offensive dominance throughout his career in the OHL. His high-end playmaking ability and hockey smarts compliment his natural abilities as a center, but he has demonstrated, especially this season, a keen ability to put the puck in the net.

Seguin has not played on as strong a team as some of the other projected top picks. His ability to still put up points in bunches and help the Whalers continue to win hockey games has been impressive.

Seguin might just be the smartest player in this year's draft. He also plays down the middle, has good size, and the skating ability to translate very smoothly to the NHL level. Seguin has fantastic vision on the ice coupled with a very high hockey I.Q. He has very soft hands and has NHL caliber scoring ability to go along with his elite playmaking skills that makes players around him better.

Tyler also serves as one of the leaders in the Whalers room, adding to his resume as arguably the most complete player in this year's draft.

PROJECTION

Seguin projects to be a top line center in the NHL and should make an impact early in his career. Seguin could be drafted as early as the top pick in the 2010 draft.

Taylor Hall

Center - Windsor (OHL)
Born Nov 14, 1991 Kingston, ONT
Height 6.00 Weight 180 Shoots L

SCOUTING REPORT

The favorite to be the #1 pick for two years now, Windsor Spitfires forward Taylor Hall hasn't done anything to hurt his chances this season. Hall was the only draft eligible player to make Team Canada's World Junior Championship roster and averaged two points a game at the famous tourney.

In terms of ability, Hall has elite speed. His first few steps are world class and that ability combined with his never say die attitude, makes Hall a nightmare for opposing defenders. He's fantastic at closing the gap on the forecheck and, as demonstrated by his stats, is an elite scorer. Furthermore, no one wants the puck on the ice more than Hall, and he simply never stops competing. This was never more evident than in Hall leading Windsor on their 2008-2009 Memorial Cup run, as well as taking on some very big and strong defenders at the WJC. Although seen as more of a scorer then playmaker, Hall has shown an ever-increasing ability to distribute the puck, which is reflected well in his statistics. In terms of things to work on, Hall needs to be a bit more consistent on the defensive side of his game. It's improving but he sometimes breaks down in coverage in his own end. Hall can also have games where he holds on to the puck and over-handles it a bit. This leads to some unforced turnovers.

PROJECTION

Hall projects to be a top-line, impact player early in his NHL career. With his speed, he shouldn't have much trouble adjusting to the pace of the NHL game, and with his compete level, you know he is up for the challenge of the NHL. Hall is all but a lock to be one of the first two players taken in this year's draft.

Erik Gudbranson

Defense - Kingston (OHL)
Born Jan 7 1992 Orleans, ONT
Height 6.03 Weight 195 Shoots R

SCOUTING REPORT

Eric Gudbranson, a towering defenseman from Kingston of the OHL, could end up being the best defenseman taken from this year's draft crop. Although injuries derailed his season and his potential appearance in the CHL top prospects game, Gudbranson still remains a top prospect in this draft.

Gudbranson's character is unquestionable. He possesses all the traits one likes in a player: He is a leader, very composed and poised on the ice, mature, smart, and has future captain written all over him. In terms of his ability, he has a rocket shot, which has helped increase his offensive production. He makes crisp, smart first passes, and can contribute in all three zones. For a guy of his size, Gudbranson is a smooth skater. Finally, he has innate hockey sense that rivals many of the top picks in the draft. Although there is still room for improvement in his physical game, Gudbranson has shown huge strides in this regard this season. He is also not opposed to dropping the gloves when necessary.

PROJECTION

Erik is not quite the skater that Cam Fowler is but that's not a knock, as he is still a fantastic skater. There might not be anyone is in this draft who is as strong a skater as Fowler. We rate Gudbranson, with his frame, skills and skating as the most NHL ready defenseman in this draft. We also think he has the most overall potential. Throw in this kid's character and one doesn't need to worry too much whether or not he will work his way up to reach that potential. HockeyProspect.com pegs Gudbranson as a potential #1 NHL Defenseman.

Brett Connolly

LW - Prince George (WHL)
Born May 2 1992 Prince George, BC
Height 6.02 Weight 181 Shoots R

SCOUTING REPORT

Although his 2009-2010 campaign was mired by injuries, winger Brett Connolly remains a top prospect in the 2010 draft. Connolly is known for being the first 16 year old to score 30 goals in a WHL season since Patrick Marleau's 1995-1996 campaign. In fact, his rookie campaign was so fantastic it leaves him a top prospect despite his struggling to get on the ice this season. His previous success has cemented him as the top WHL prospect for this year's draft.

Connolly is a sniper in the every sense of the word. His release and shot are as good as it gets and quite accurate. He possesses a power forward frame, which he should be able to fill out to round out his game. He may not be the prettiest skater in the draft, but Connolly doesn't struggle to get from Point A to Point B. Finally, he has the innate ability to find the right areas of the ice to score. He possesses the so-called "knack" that separates good shooters from good scorers.

PROJECTION

We are very high this player. If not for injury concerns (our experience with his type of injury has not been good), we would probably be talking about Connolly in the same breath as Hall and Seguin. Connolly has all the tools and brings it game in and game out. He's a huge kid who puts up points in bunches. Top end snipers with size like this are not plentiful. He has NHL written all over him. We can only hope that his injuries, which might even see his draft stock drop far enough to push him out of the top ten, don't derail his progress in becoming a formidable NHL sniper. Connolly has the ability to be a 30-35 goal man in the NHL.

Cam Fowler

Defense - Windsor (OHL)
Born Dec 5, 1991 Farmington Hills, MI
Height 6.02 Weight 190 Shoots L

SCOUTING REPORT

Cam Fowler, a United States born defenseman, who turned down an NCAA opportunity in order to join the Memorial Cup Champion Windsor Spitfires, could be the next in what has been a great infusion of American defensemen into recent drafts. Fowler had a great season for Windsor, and put his skills on display as he led the US World Junior Championship team to a gold medal this year. Many commended his performance against teammate and top prospect Taylor Hall throughout the tournament.

Fowler has all the tools one needs to be a great defenseman. He is an unbelievably smooth skater (one of the best in this draft), and possesses fantastic speed. He is quite agile in the defensive end, and his skating makes him a valuable contributor on the rush and in the offensive zone. He has a good shot that can be quite potent on the power play. Fowler has a good frame, and adding muscle will make his defensive game stronger. His defensive game isn't perfect, but certainly not something he can't improve on. We see his weakness as being tentative as far as playing the body and physical play in general. We think he takes a long route to the puck at times, and rushes some plays on occasion if he sees a big hit coming. It won't show up as much now but could in the NHL if not corrected.

PROJECTION

Like all young defensemen, Fowler has some room to develop (especially his physical play in his own end). However, he has all the tools, and might get more confident as he gets stronger. He could be a top tier defenseman and a star player in the NHL, if he can develop the physical part of his game.

Vladimir Tarasenko

RW - Novosibirsk Siber (KHL)
Born Dec 13 1991, Russia
Height 6.00 Weight 192 Shoots L

SCOUTING REPORT

The best the KHL has to offer this draft, Vladimir Tarasenko (son of the great Andrei Tarasenko), is a highly skilled Russian winger. Tarasenko put up good numbers this season in the KHL, while playing consistent minutes.

Tarasenko, like many Russian players, is great with his stick. He knows how to make things happen and his hands are considered as good as anyone in the draft. Obviously with hands like his, Tarasenko has no problem making plays, and should be a steady point producer at the next level.

In terms of improvements, there are a couple things Tarasenko could do to round out his game. He is a good skater, but could stand to work on his acceleration. His consistency across the ice needs to improve, especially if he wants to be an impact NHL player. Finally, he has room to grow with his play without the puck. Still, with his compete level, there is no reason to think Tarasenko won't round out his game to make the jump to the NHL.

PROJECTION

Should Tarasenko work on some of his weaknesses, there is no reason to think he won't be an impact offensive force in the NHL. We expect he will fall down the draft board on draft day due to the risk currently involved with selecting many Russian players.

Brandon Gormley

Defense - Moncton (QMJHL)
Born Feb 18 1992 Murray River, PEI
Height 6.01 Weight 175 Shoots L

SCOUTING REPORT

A former #1 overall pick in the QMJHL draft, Brandon Gormley continues to be looked at as one of the top three defensemen in the draft along with Cam Fowler and Eric Gudbranson. After a solid first season with Moncton, Gormley improved his offensive numbers this season. Gormley is quite solid in all zones. His skating is superb, with a strong and smooth stride. He is not exactly a puck rusher, but makes the right pass, and, in the offensive zone, has a heavy, accurate shot that he is able to keep low for deflections or rebounds. His shot and ability to make the right play is especially helpful on the power play, where Gormley is a very capable quarterback. In terms of defensive play, Gormley isn't an intimidating physical presence, but is incredibly smart, knows how to position himself and always makes the right play.

Overall, Gormley is a player that plays with a ton of poise and confidence in his game. His skating ability and intelligence leaves Gormley with a lot of potential.

PROJECTION

With his skill-set and intelligence, Gormley has great NHL potential. He could easily be a top pairing defenseman on a team, and should at least be a top three player. Gormley could be a top five draft pick depending on team's needs.

Alexander Burmistrov

Center - Barrie (OHL)
Born Oct 21, 1991 Kazan, Russia
Height 6.00 Weight 170 Shoots L

SCOUTING REPORT

Russian-Born Alexander Burmistrov joined the Barrie Colts for the 2009-2010 campaign. A point per game player at the OHL level, Burmistrov showed off his elite sniper abilities throughout the season.

Burmistrov brought a high-end skill package from Russia to the Colts. He has a great shot and is incredibly shifty on his skates, showing great ability to turn on a dime and shake opponents. He can protect the puck well enough for his size, but should get better as he grows in size and strength. He also proved to be a formidable player on the power play. Still, Burmistrov has some weaknesses to address in order to succeed at the next level. He must make sure he shows up to play every night, and distribute the puck more. His puck skills are amazing and when he has the puck it's tough to get it from him. One Assistant Coach says, "He is the hardest worker on the team." It's not uncommon to see him working on his game after practice. We would like to see him improve his consistency from shift to shift. Burmistrov has improved his five-on-five play drastically throughout the season, and works hard in the defensive zone.

PROJECTION

With Burmistrov, it'll be a matter of maturing his game in order for him to be a high-end top 6 NHL contributor. The skills and skating ability are certainly there, but if there is a risk (apart from the usual concerns regarding Russians), it is whether his mental game develops to provide consistency at an appropriate NHL level. Should it develop, he has the potential to be a high end scoring line player in the NHL. With his skills and recent improvements, we rate Burmistrov no worse than a mid first round pick.

Nino Niederreiter

LW - Portland (WHL)
Born Sep 8, 1992 Chur, Switzerland
Height 6.02 Weight 203 Shoots L

SCOUTING REPORT

Rising rapidly up the draft rankings since his valiant World Junior Championship performance (highlighted by his "you can't stop me" performance against the Russians), Swiss-born winger Nino Niederreiter has become one of the top prospects in this year's draft. Niederreiter boasts good size, and already knows how to use it to protect the puck. His work along the walls is fantastic and his impeccable balance contributes to his high rate of success in one-on-one battles. Nino understands how to cycle the puck down low and uses excellent body positioning in this regard. Like many WHL players, Niederreiter plays with some serious grit and never stops competing or bringing the intensity. This has been evident by his great play in big games. Finally, and this is what really sets Nino apart from many other prospects, is how creative he is with the puck for a big guy. He has good hands and is a proven goal scorer at every level. All his skills, coupled with his character makeup will make Nino an attractive winger for any NHL GM come draft day.

PROJECTION

At the beginning of the season, Niederreiter looked like someone that would go between the 15th to 30th pick, however, with his play since December, he may not make it past #10 depending on team needs. Niederreiter has first line potential in the NHL.

Nick Bjugstad

Center - Blaine High School
Born 1992 Coon Rapids, Minnesota
Height 6.05 Weight 190 Shoots R

SCOUTING REPORT

Nick Bjugstad, who recently completed his season at Blaine High School in Minnesota, should be the highest drafted USA High School player in the draft. To top off his stellar season at Blaine, Bjugstad was recently named Mr. Hockey in Minnesota, a highly prestigious award given previously to players such as Paul Martin (New Jersey Devils), Nick Leddy (Minnesota prospect), and Ryan McDonagh (New York Rangers prospect). Bjugstad is committed to the University of Minnesota for the fall of 2010. His uncle, Scott Bjugstad, was also an NHL player.

Bjugstad draws many comparisons to other big Minnesota kids, such as Blake Wheeler and David Backes. Bjugstad plays a highly skilled, character game and is learning how to use his size to his advantage. He has also been praised for his good work ethic and leadership qualities on the ice. There isn't much Bjugstad can't do on the ice. He knows how to put the puck in the net, has elite playmaking ability, and is learning how to use his body. However, like many players at his size and age, Bjugstad will need to learn to use his body even more effectively as he continues to take on bigger and stronger competition. His challenges won't be unlike those Wheeler faced as a Golden Gopher.

PROJECTION

Obviously, Bjugstad's current league competition hasn't been the same as other top prospects in the draft, leading him to be a bit more of a wildcard. However, he will be playing in one of the toughest conferences in NCAA hockey, with past success in grooming solid NHL players. With his size, skill-set, and credentials, Bjugstad should be a top 20 pick.

Jeff Skinner

Center - Kitchener (OHL)
Born May 16, 1992 Markham, ONT
Height 5.10 Weight 182 Shoots L

SCOUTING REPORT

Jeff Skinner has been a HockeyProspect.com favorite for some time now. He almost went the NCAA route but instead has been a standout for Kitchener of the OHL. Looking at his numbers, you would think Skinner should be a sure-fire top ten pick. In fact, his goal scoring numbers rival those of Hall, Seguin, or any other top pick.

Unfortunately, unlike Hall and Seguin, Skinner is not quite an elite skater yet. He also needs to improve his play in his own end. Nonetheless, Skinner isn't lazy and certainly competes on a nightly basis. What makes Skinner so appealing is his pure goal scoring ability. His numbers don't lie. Skinner knows how to put the puck in the net and ranks among the top of the class in that part of the game. At 5'10", Skinner has a frame to translate to the NHL, but he will need some time to get stronger. What Skinner has that most prospects don't, is the "it" factor. He knows where to go to put the puck in the net and how to finish the play. He is willing to do whatever it takes to make that happen.

PROJECTION

Skinner could turn out to be one of the biggest steals of this draft. Again, he will need to add on size to his 5'10" frame, but he thinks the game and finishes at a high level. Skinner has raised his draft stock with a huge playoff run. At print time he already has 18 playoff goals. We think Skinner will go no later than the middle of the first round, and has the potential to be a goal scoring threat at the NHL level.

Mikael Granlund

Center - Karpat, Finland
Born Feb 26 1992
Height 5.10 Weight 172 Shoots L

SCOUTING REPORT

Mikael Granlund is a skilled Finnish forward who most recently played in one of the elite European leagues (SM-Liiga) where he averaged nearly a point per game. It has been tough to get a read on Granlund. Although he is clearly putting up numbers in Europe, HockeyProspect.com would have liked to see a more impressive World Junior Championship performance.

Although not a big player, Granlund plays beyond his size, and battles along the walls and behind the net. He is only an average skater, which along with his size are our biggest concerns. Granlund has good balance and possesses great vision in the offensive zone. His game resembles that of Marc Savard, with his vision and playmaking ability, whether it is playing on the half wall on the power play or floating a pass to a streaking teammate, the resemblance can't be denied. He is pretty much a pass first player, but has the hands to score some nifty goals as well. To succeed in the NHL, Granlund is going to need to continue to play beyond his size and not back down from NHL defensemen.

PROJECTION

Granlund may not make an instant impact in the NHL, but he has the hands and vision to be an impact offensive player. Eventually, if he improves his skating, he would be a handful on the power play.

Although we don't see Granlund as a great skater, he is elite in so many areas that we are forcing ourselves to ignore both the skating issues and the lack of size. We do hope he is indeed his listed 5'10". The NHL combine where he could be measured takes place after we publish.

Jack Campbell

Goalie - USA NTDP (USHL)
Born Jan 9 1992 Port Huron, MI
Height 6.01 Weight 171 Catches Left

SCOUTING REPORT

Jack Campbell is the cream of the crop in terms of goaltenders for this year's draft. The U.S born net-minder is a product of the U.S National Development program, and plans on playing for the OHL's Windsor Spitfires next season. He has excelled in many big tournaments including in relief for the WJC gold medal game and standing on his head against Canada. His most recent success had come in Belarus where at print time he has lead team USA to the Gold Medal final.

HockeyProspect.com is very high on Campbell's skill set. He's already proven to be a big game goalie, and at a young age possesses an NHL ready frame. He is a quick goaltender despite his size, and clearly has the mental toughness/resilience that any successful NHL goalie needs. He has strong lateral movement and is developing nice habits in terms of playing various angles. Finally, his rebound control is excellent and his glove is very solid.

PROJECTION

As we all know, the development of goaltenders can be tricky. Still, we can't help but be excited about Campbell's potential. There is not much to dislike when you take a hard look at Campbell's resume. With his mental toughness, and progression to date, he looks as safe a bet as you will find to become an NHL goalie. Based on team needs, Campbell should be a first round pick, and we put his value as a top 20 pick.

Jaden Schwartz

Forward - Tri City Storm (USHL)
Born Jun 25 1992 Wilcox, SASK
Height 5.10 Weight 193 Shoots L

SCOUTING REPORT

Jaden Schwartz is a Saskatchewan born forward who most recently played for Tri-City of the USHL. He isn't the biggest player in the league, but had no problem putting up tons of points as a complete offensive force after joining the USHL. Schwartz will be joining Colorado College of the NCAA powerhouse WCHA conference next fall. He was also a member of the Canadian U-18 team at the Ivan Hlinka tournament.

Schwartz is productive on the offensive end of the ice because of his uncanny vision. He can slow the play down and make the right, creative play. However, he also has the dynamic factor in his game, where he can dangle around opponents and make it look easy. Despite his offensive prowess, Schwartz also competes on the defensive end and is willing to do whatever it takes to win. If he could improve his foot-speed, Schwartz could become even more dynamic by adding a transition game to his offensive toolbox. In the end, what Schwartz needs to improve on most would be his foot-speed. Attending an NCAA program will undoubtedly help him add on the necessary strength and we will have to wait and see regarding his foot-speed.

PROJECTION

Schwartz projects to be a creative, play-making NHL forward who could be deadly on the power play. The attribute we like best about him is the combination of his skill and all out effort every shift. We always look a bit closer at players who are on the smallish side but when they have the ability that Schwartz possesses the size concern is eliminated quickly. 1st Rounder.

Mark Pysyk

Defense – Edmonton (WHL)
Born Jan 11 1992 Sherwood Pk. ALTA
Height 6.00 Weight 170 Shoots R

SCOUTING REPORT

A member of the Edmonton Oil Kings of the WHL, Mark Pysyk has steadily improved each season and is one of the stronger defense candidates in the upcoming draft. Pysyk played in the CHL Top Prospects game this year, as well as being a member of the 2009 Canadian U-18 roster.

Pysyk is a lunch-box type. He shows up and does his job defensively, despite playing on a relatively weak team. He got big minutes this season and excelled in those minutes. He plays with toughness and has no trouble getting in shooting lanes to block the puck. Has shown offensive improvement in each season in the WHL and can make the right first pass, as well as rush the puck.

Pysyk has struggled a bit with his pivots, leaving him susceptible to some speedsters. Overall, his foot speed could use some improvement. Sizewise, while not huge, Pysyk has the frame to make it at the next level. Like any young player, he could stand to add some strength to his game. Pysyk certainly has NHL potential.

PROJECTION

Having all the tools, despite needing some improvement, Pysyk certainly has a future in the NHL. Should he add some strength to his frame, and some speed as well, Pysyk stands to be a steady, top-4 defenseman at the next level.

Pysyk should be a top 15 pick in the draft and might even find himself in the top 10.

Derek Forbort

Defense - USA NTDP (USHL)
Born Mar 4 1992 Duluth, MN
Height 6.04 Weight 195 Shoots L

SCOUTING REPORT

A big, skilled defenseman that can contribute on both ends of the ice, Derek Forbort most recently skated with the US National Development U-18 team, and will attend NCAA powerhouse North Dakota next season. The Minnesota-born player has risen from a mid-round prospect to a top defensive prospect.

Forbort possesses an NHL frame, with room to put on some muscle and make himself a physical mis-match for any forwards. He is a great skater for his size, with nice agility. He is a solid puck-mover that can rush the puck up the ice, but consistently makes the correct first pass. His stay at home game and puck-moving game is great. However, he could stand to improve offensively. Hopefully some training at an elite University like North Dakota, can help him out in that end. Still, with his size and skating ability, Forbort is an exciting prospect.

PROJECTION

With some offensive improvement, Forbort could become a top pairing defenseman. Right now his size and skating ability are enough to make Forbort a viable prospect. Forbort will go in the first round of the draft, and could be a top 15 pick. He should rise to be a top 4 defenseman in the NHL.

Ryan Johansen

Forward - Portland (WHL)
Born Jul 31, 1992 Port Moody, BC
Height 6.02 Weight 180 Shoots R

SCOUTING REPORT

After one season in the BCHL, Ryan Johansen joined the Portland Winterhawks of the WHL this season and made his presence known immediately. He was basically a point per game player, and contributed on all ends of the ice for the Winterhawks. While many fans watch the Winterhawks for Swiss Sensation Nino Niederreiter, Johansen has caught many a scout's eye with his impressive play. Johansen also turned down NCAA offers in order to play in the WHL.

To put it simply, Johansen is big and skilled with room to get even bigger. He has a good shot, but is also an impressive playmaker. He has a flair for the dramatic as well, scoring an elusive coast-to-coast goal this season against Everett. He is very driven, and works hard on all facets of his game. He also knows how to use his size to his advantage, and does some little things on the ice that are impossible to teach.

PROJECTION

We are very impressed with Johansen's game. To put it lightly, there isn't much there to dislike. He doesn't have the resume that some of the other top picks have, but Johansen is making quite a name for himself. He could be an absolute steal in the middle of the first round of the draft and has top end potential/size.

Emerson Etem

Center - Medicine Hat (WHL)
Born Jun 16, 1992 Long Beach, CA
Height 6.00 Weight 194 Shoots L

SCOUTING REPORT

Originally a product of the U.S. National Development team, Etem has since joined Medicine Hat of the WHL and put together quite an impressive season. Etem did a good job getting used to his new surroundings and had little problem adjusting to the pace of the Western Hockey League. Etem has done such a good job of blending right into the WHL that he has surpassed the expectations of most fans and even coaches.

Etem's game is built around speed. He uses his top-notch skating ability to gain space on opposing defensemen, protect the puck and create opportunities. Although he can stick handle in tight spaces, Etem is most productive by using his speed and puck control to get to the net and let off a quick shot. Etem is a high end goal scorer who seldom misses chances around the net. He is very solid on his skates and is dangerous almost every shift. Emerson is a smart hockey player who sees the ice pretty well and has made great strides in just about every facet of his game this season.

Etem will need to clean up his play in his own end a little bit but it's not too uncommon to see younger players struggle at times on the defensive side of the puck.

PROJECTION

Etem certainly has the speed and offensive ability to be a productive NHL player. Whether or not he is a 3rd line center or 1st line will depend on how well he develops his overall game. With his attitude and natural leadership ability, it is safe to say that Etem could slide into a 3rd line NHL Role, but his speed makes top-end potential a definite possibility.

Austin Watson

Right Wing - Peterborough (OHL)
Born Jan 13, 1992 Ann Arbor, MI
Height 6.03 Weight 171 Shoots R

SCOUTING REPORT

Michigan-born born Austin Watson was a member of the reigning Memorial Cup Champion Windsor Spitfires, before being traded to Peterborough late this season. He has also been on the United States U-18 select roster and was a second round pick in the OHL draft. The first thing that sticks out about Watson is his size. He is huge at 6'3 and should be able to add plenty of muscle to his frame.

Despite his size, Watson is a good skater and doesn't look like a lumbering big man out on the ice. What Watson brings to the ice is a mature, three-zone game. He is a complete player and does what he needs to do to try and win games. He is great on the penalty kill and has no problem getting down on the ice to block shots (as exemplified in the CHL top prospects game). Just like blocking shots, he excels at doing many of the little things that go into winning a game. This versatility makes him a viable player in any situation and on any line. Although not proving to be an offensive powerhouse, Watson has improved greatly since joining the OHL, and certainly knows how to put the puck in the net.

PROJECTION

Watson is a viable NHL prospect. We would like to see him play up to his size a little more often in order to help his professional aspirations. Still, if his offensive game continues to develop, and he sticks with his consistent three-zone play, he could make it as a top player in the NHL. Austin will be a pretty solid pickup for some lucky team in the draft.

Tyler Toffoli

Right Wing – Ottawa (OHL)
Born Apr 24, 1992 Scarborough, ONT
Height 6.00 Weight 181 Shoots R

SCOUTING REPORT

Tyler Toffoli is a Scarborough Ontario-born right-winger who played his second season with the Ottawa 67's this year. He had a great season, averaging more than a point per game, and won himself a spot in the CHL Top Prospects game. He also dramatically improved his point totals from his first OHL season to his second.

HockeyProspect.com has seen Toffoli play since PeeWee. He has always had great hockey sense and vision, both of which rank near the top in this year's draft class. His vision/hockey sense help him to be a terrific passer, which can make people around him look like stars. His skating has also shown improvement since he entered the OHL. If he can get his skating to an even higher level, it should elevate his game greatly. We like the improvement he has shown in all three zones throughout his hockey career. One more thing he needs to improve on is his strength/grit in the dirty areas of the ice. Added size would surely help him out in this regard.

PROJECTION

Toffoli has about as much hockey sense and vision as any other member of the draft class. Should his strength and skating ability improve, Toffoli's game could really take off. Hockey-Prospect.com considers Tyler a mid first-round prospect, and we feel he could be a steal if taken in the bottom of the round.

Dylan McIlrath

Defense - Moose Jaw (WHL)
Born Apr 20 1992 Winnipeg, MAN
Height 6.05 Weight 215 Shoots R

SCOUTING REPORT

Dylan McIlrath is one of the more interesting prospects in this year's draft class. He is certainly one of the meanest as well, a strong and imposing defenseman for Moose Jaw of the Western Hockey League. McIlrath has made waves for his old school play and gained a fan in Bobby Orr by getting into a fight in the CHL Top Prospects game.

Calling McIlrath an old school defenseman may be putting it too lightly. He is mean and almost nasty on the ice, playing with tons of grit every shift. However, despite routinely hitting, punishing, and fighting opponents (all at the age of 17) McIlrath has developed his overall game immensely. He is great in his own zone, is getting better in the neutral and offensive zones, and is earning more and more minutes for Moose Jaw. Not surprisingly, McIlrath has developed a booming shot. The 6'5", 215 lb McIlrath defines a solid, tough to play against player. You don't see many defensemen who can be near 200 PIM's and still be a productive player, but McIlrath does it.

PROJECTION

One thing we know is McIlrath has the size, determination and toughness to be an NHL defenseman. However, it is what type of defenseman that remains to be seen. Could he turn into a top pairing, team leader type player? Absolutely. However, he could also end up as more of a bottom-pairing player. Still, he is a unique prospect in that he has the toughness, but also potential. He could be the defenceman's version of Milan Lucic and will likely go in the late first or early second round.

Riley Sheahan

Forward - Notre Dame (NCAA)
Born Dec 7, 1991 St. Catharine's, ONT
Height 6.02 Weight 200 Shoots L

SCOUTING REPORT

Riley Sheahan looks to be the top NCAA draft prospect this season. Playing for Notre Dame, the Canadian born Sheahan was a contributor in just his first season for the Fighting Irish. We also watched him play quite a few games in Junior B before he headed off to Notre Dame where he dominated at times against inferior talent. We would have liked to have seen him play a more physical game.

This season was not a great success for Notre Dame and the team's pure trap system did not allow Sheahan to fully display his offensive ability. However, we don't think this will affect his draft status too negatively.

Sheahan is quite a skilled player. He has good size, but that size has not adversely affected his skating, as he has a smooth stride and good speed. He is not the most natural goal scorer, but has the ability to create tons of opportunities for himself. He also is quite strong on the puck and can handle the puck well. Already a big, strong player, with more time to gain strength in the NCAA schedule, Sheahan could be quite a physical force when he leaves the NCAA.

PROJECTION

It is hard to judge Sheahan's game this season. He was a natural freshman, playing with much older players, in a system that doesn't allow players to thrive offensively. However, we do know that Sheahan will leave NCAA hockey with a strong, balanced game and NHL size. Therefore, Riley still looks to be a middle of the first round talent with good NHL upside.

Brock Nelson

Center - Warroad (HS)
Born 10/15/1991 Warroad, MN
Height 6.03 Weight 205 Shoots L

SCOUTING REPORT

Brock Nelson is another towering Minnesota high school player eligible for the draft. He recently completed his season for Warroad High School and is arguably the second best Minnesota prospect in the draft, just barely behind Nick Bjugstad. Nelson was also a finalist for the prestigious Mr. Hockey Award and scouts love that he is attending powerhouse North Dakota of the WCHA next season. His uncle also happens to be

Dave Christian, a famed member of the United States 1980 Miracle on Ice team.

Nelson is a committed player at both ends of the ice. He skates extremely well for a big player, with top end acceleration. This acceleration, combined with his size allows him to effortlessly beat defenders and get in a good position to let off his cannon of a shot. In the offensive zone, he really has the complete package of speed, size, and soft hands that many Minnesota-born forwards possess. Still, he has yet to play against the true top competition of the world, so how he fares at UND will have a lot to do with his growth as a player.

PROJECTION

Just like Bjugstad, with his size, skill-set, and three-zone play, the sky is truly the limit for Nelson. He is already putting himself in a favorable position by attending North Dakota next season. Not playing against the top competition in the world this season will likely keep Nelson out of the top 15-20, but he could go anywhere from 20-35 in the draft. With development, he projects to be top six forward. His game lends itself more to a sniping, committed power forward rather than just a playmaker.

Quinton Howden

Left Wing - Moose Jaw (WHL)
Born Jan 21, 1992 Oak Bank, MAN
Height 6.03 Weight 183 Shoots L

SCOUTING REPORT

Quinton Howden, a forward for Moose Jaw, who recently completed his second full season in the WHL, brings obvious NHL size to the draft. He has a good frame and plenty of room to add muscle. After going through an adjustment period in his first season in the WHL, Howden ramped up his offensive production, becoming a point per game player this season. However, one could not have expected too much out of Howden his first season, playing on such a poor team.

Howden is a fairly complete offensive player. He can score goals and distributes the puck well. He also skates with top end speed for a big player. He is also not afraid to crash and bang to win battles for pucks. Finally, while not spectacular, Howden does have above average vision and hockey sense.

Before this season, one could consider Howden's play away from the puck and in the defensive zone as a weakness. However, he has drastically improved this portion of his game, becoming a solid two-way player. He is developing a great awareness of what to do in the defensive zone.

PROJECTION

With his size and skating ability, Howden is a good prospect. He has only put up numbers for one season, which will probably keep him out of the top 20 of the draft. That said, he has the size, and ability to be a scoring line player in the NHL, and is a very good, late first round pick.

Tyler Pitlick

Forward - Minnesota St. U (NCAA)
Born Nov 1 1991 Centerville, MN
Height 6.01 Weight 190 Shoots R

SCOUTING REPORT

A 2009 finalist for the Minnesota Mr. Hockey award (won by Wild prospect Nick Leddy and formerly by other big prospects such as Ryan McDonagh, Aaron Ness and Brian Lee, as well as current NHL Paul Martin), Tyler Pitlick played this season at Minnesota State in the NCAA powerhouse WCHA conference. He also previously played on the United States Under 17 and Under 18 teams.

Pitlick is an offensive horse. He is extremely creative with the puck, but is smart with his passes as well. His offensive abilities can be attributed to his solid vision, combined with tantalizing hands. He really knows how to put the puck in the net. Pitlick being such a threat makes the players around him better. Like many players at this age, he has some maturing to do in terms of his play without the puck and passing, but his natural ability to put the puck in the net will not go unnoticed in this draft. He can dangle, shoot, and score, and has good size to translate to the next level.

PROJECTION

HockeyProspect.com believes Pitlick may translate better as a center, but should he continue to mature, Pitlick should be a nice scorer at the NHL level.

Maxim Kitsyn

Forward - Metallurg (KHL)
Born Dec 24 1991
Height 6.02 Weight 192

SCOUTING REPORT

Maxim Kitsyn, a winger who most recently played with Metallurg of the KHL is clearly blessed with a pro size frame. At 6'2 and 185 pounds, he can be a force on the wing. He has yet to play in North America, so, to understand his potential, you have to look past his slightly lackluster stats in the KHL, and see his strengths.

What makes Kitsyn an intriguing prospect is the fact that he is a multi-faceted offensive weapon.

He has the size and strength to be versatile, and he has no problem doing so. He can score a goal by skating down the wing, undressing two defensemen and using his good shot to snipe it, or he can park his big body in front of the net and score an ugly one. He has improved his skating aggressively since joining the KHL and also is getting better with physical play. Right now, however, he is most effective when the ice opens up for him.

A troubling aspect about Kitsyn's game is his weak defensive play. Unfortunately, Kitsyn was so used to dominating opponents with his size, that he didn't learn the defensive game. Since he joined the KHL, it has been a struggle in that regard. He could also stand to distribute the puck more.

PROJECTION

Kitsyn is the classic case of a player blessed with all the tools, but needs to round out his game. He also has the fact that he is Russian and has yet to set foot on North American soil working against him in terms of draft status. This may keep him out of the top ten, but Kitsyn should go between pick 10 and 30 and could develop into a very capable power forward.

Stanislav Galiev

Forward - St. John (QMJHL)
Born Jan 17, 1992 Moscow, Russia
Height 6.01 Weight 177 Shoots R

SCOUTING REPORT

After playing one season in the USHL, Stanislav Galiev joined the QMJHL this season as a member of the Saint John squad. Although his stats were not quite as gaudy as in the USHL, Galiev proved himself to be a dynamic offensive player in the highest level of competition. Unfortunately, he was not on Russia's World Junior Championship team, so we didn't get to view him in the truly elite tournament.

Galiev has good size, and has a great offensive skill set. He is an unreal playmaker, and that is truly where his offensive prowess lies. He makes creative passes and has the vision to use his uncanny skills. Obviously with this skill, he is quite capable of running a power play. He also works hard for the puck in the offensive zone. He is also quite a speedster and can absolutely fly, once he gets his legs moving. He has also improved his willingness to go into the high traffic areas.

There are a couple aspects of his game that Galiev could stand to improve. First, he needs to shoot more. He has a quick, hard release and the ability to put the puck in the net. If he would shoot more, it would open up even more passing lanes for the crafty playmaker. Also, just like many young forwards, his play away from the puck leaves some to be desired.

PROJECTION

What it comes down to for Galiev is being able to find room for himself to make these passes. That will require shooting more and spending more time in the high traffic areas. Galiev could be a potent point producer in the NHL.

Beau Bennett

Forward – Penticton (BCHL)
Born November 27, 1991 Gardena, CA
Height 6.01 Weight 180 Shoots R

SCOUTING REPORT

Beau Bennett, a California-born forward dominated the BCHL this season as his draft status soared. He was the first rookie in seven years to record 100 points and is drawing tons of comparisons to Maple Leaf forward Tyler Bozak, except Bennett is accomplishing all of this at the age of 18 rather than 20. Like Bozak, Bennett will attend NCAA powerhouse Denver next season.

Bennett has a nice 6'1" frame, but could stand to add some strength to it. However, being on the NCAA schedule should help him out in this regard. He is quite impressive on the offensive end and makes you say "wow" a lot when he is on the ice. He is a great playmaker along with being a high-end scorer. He accomplishes much of his production in the cycle game and with his intelligence, rather than him just beating various defensemen one-on-one. His skating is solid, but not game breaking, which further highlights his natural offensive ability. He is simply dangerous on every shift on the ice.

Obviously, when it comes to Tier Two players, it's hard to compare them to Major Junior players, as the competition is so different. Even saying that, Bennett is a player we really like at Hockey-Prospect.com

PROJECTION

As Bennett plays at Denver, he should get stronger and stronger. However, he is not much of a gritty player, so his development may be scoring line forward or nothing. Still, with the way coaches and scouts speak of Bennett, he looks to be a top 40 talent in the draft

Jon Merrill

Defense - USA NTDP (USHL)
Born Feb 3 1992 -- Brighton, MI
Height 6.03 Weight 205 Shoots L

SCOUTING REPORT

Jon Merrill, who played for the U.S. National Development team, is a huge defenseman committed to the University of Michigan for the 2010 season. He has all the tools required to be a good NHL defenseman. However, it was a rocky season for Merrill off the ice, leading to a potential drop in his draft status.

Skill-wise, Merrill has what he needs. He is a

huge kid, and has a Chris Pronger-esque element to his game. In the defensive zone, he uses his stick well, wins the battles and displays good coverage. He can lug the puck up the ice with his smooth skating stride or make the right first pass to get it out of the zone. Once in the offensive zone, he has a soft set of hands and a hard slap shot from the point. Clearly, Merrill has the toolbox to be a successful NHL defenseman.

Merrill is a true talent. It will be interesting to see how his suspension from the US National Development team this season will impact his draft day. That is not something you want to see if you are an NHL team.

PROJECTION

We won't deny that Merrill has the tools. His development at Michigan will be interesting, as other defensemen coming out of Michigan have had mixed success in the NHL. Merrill needs to focus in on the start to his NCAA career. He will have plenty of time to develop more as a player and prove that he is an NHL blue chip prospect. He could go late in the first round or early in the second round.

Stephen Johns

Defense - USA NTDP (USHL)
Born Apr 18 1992 Wampum, PA
Height 6.03 Weight 220 Shoots R

SCOUTING REPORT

Stephen Johns is a big defenseman who recently completed a two-year stint with the U.S. National Development team. He has enough size and strength already to play in the NHL. He isn't going to be the type of player that is a huge factor in the offensive zone, but is a steady defenseman. We are still waiting to see if Johns will attend the NCAA's Notre Dame or Windsor of the OHL.

Johns plays defense exactly the way a big player

should. He plays simple, using his size effectively to make an impact against opposing forwards. He is a hard to play against on the walls, knows how to position himself and certainly has a solid amount of defensive awareness. His hockey IQ is high for someone his age and immensely valuable. He makes smart, crisp outlet passes, and has an overall mature game for his age.

Right now, it looks like Johns has limited offensive upside. We will have to see how he develops on that end of the ice.

PROJECTION

Johns should be able to develop his game enough to be a top four defenseman in the league. His size should limit some growing pains as he learns how to play defense at a higher level. His offensive progression will make a big impact on what kind of defenseman he is in the NHL. He could be a #3 or #4 or perhaps develop into a legitimate shutdown player. We see Johns as a late first or very early second round pick.

Greg McKegg

Center - Erie (OHL)
Born Jun 17, 1992 St. Thomas, ONT
Height 6.00 Weight 185 Shoots L

SCOUTING REPORT

After a slow first season for the Erie Otters of the Ontario Hockey League, Greg McKegg took off this season with an offensive explosion. In fact, HockeyProspect.com believes that playing in Erie perhaps kept McKegg under the radar, despite his impressive numbers, which consistently ranked in the top 20 of all OHL skaters.

McKegg has all the tools in the offensive zone. He has the ability to create opportunities off the rush, and also had a good shot. He has nice hockey sense, making him a great contributor playing on the half wall of a power play unit. He also distributes the puck well, keeping his offensive game balanced. Although not a huge player, McKegg is quite strong and balanced on the ice. McKegg's weakness is in his skating game. He has a choppy stride, and his first few steps are a bit weak.

PROJECTION

McKegg has the offensive tools to become a valuable contributor at the NHL level. While his season was a bit of an explosion, his improvement is noteworthy and a good sign. He will have to improve his skating to catch up with the NHL game, but it is good to see he has some natural instincts and a strong skill set. We expect the slight weakness in skating will slide him just outside of round #1 and make McKegg an early second round draft choice.

Jarred Tinordi

Defense - US NTDP (USHL)
Born Feb 20, 1992 Millersville, ND
Height 6.04 Weight 204 Shoots L

SCOUTING REPORT

The son of former NHL Mark Tinordi, Jarred Tinordi is another big defenseman coming out of the U.S. Tinordi is a similar player to Steven Johns. Like Johns, he has committed to Notre Dame to play NCAA hockey and has a nice NHL frame. However, he is a bit more raw at this point then Johns. There are rumors of Tinordi reporting to the London Knights next season. London's General Manager, Mark Hunter, missed game 7 versus Kitchener as he made a trip to Belarus for the Under-18 Tournament where Tinordi was playing.

Tinordi is a defensive d-man and hasn't displayed much of an offensive impact yet. He is a huge kid and his play in the defensive zone is very strong. He is smart, and uses his body to accomplish the little things on the ice well. He also has shown strong leadership abilities and looks to be a character player.

At first blush, it looks like Tinordi needs to improve his skating in every facet. It is reasonably good, but some foot speed and agility improvements would really help his overall game. This may be tough considering how big he is.

PROJECTION

We like Jarred's defensive game. When you combine his size, hockey IQ, character qualities, and ability to do the little things on the ice, it is quite clear that he can be effective in that end of the ice. Improvement in his skating would help him become a better-rounded prospect. Still, we think Tinordi is a valuable and safe second round pick.

Tom Kuehnhackl

RW - Landshut Cannibals
Born Jan 21 1992 Landshut, Germany
Height 6.02 Weight 170 Shoots L

SCOUTING REPORT

There is a German on his way up the prospect ranks and Kuehnhackl is his name. Kuehnhackl is currently playing with men in Germany, but next fall he will be wearing the red, white and blue of the Windsor Spitfires. The Spitfires drafted Kuehnhackl in the 2009 CHL Import Draft and after a year long wait they will get their man for the 2010/2011 OHL season.

Kuehnhackl has an NHL frame to grow into and if his father's size means anything at all, it bodes well for whatever NHL team drafts him, as dad is 6'5". Right now Tom is 6'2" and looks lanky out on the ice. He is not a player looking for open ice hits all over the ice, but he lays the body when needed and does not shy away from the rough stuff either, which is impressive when you consider he is a 1992 birth date playing against men.

Kuehnhackl is blessed with fantastic quickness in his first few steps and very good speed. He is a skilled player capable of putting the puck in the net at the NHL level. We were impressed with how well he seems to have adapted to the pro level. At this writing he has popped in 12 goals in 38 games. Former OHL'er Ryan McDonough is leading the team in scoring with 16 goals and has 4 years on young Tom.

Tom is a very smart hockey player and it shows all over the ice. His defensive zone play is quite impressive, as he makes good reads and has solid positional play. What stands out for us is his quickness for a big kid. Tom is very quick to gobble up loose pucks and did a solid job in protecting it and utilizing his long reach.

PROJECTION

Consider us fans. He may need some seasoning in the AHL after his Windsor Spitfires career is complete, but we love the raw talent this kid possesses. When you combine the hockey smarts and his willingness to get involved on every shift, we think he projects to be a top 6 forward at the NHL level.

Jordan Weal

Center – Regina Pats (WHL)
Born Apr 15 1992 North Vancouver, BC
Height 5.08 Weight 158 -Shoots R

SCOUTING REPORT

While most of the attention in Regina is focused on Team Canada star and Oiler product Jordan Eberle, small, crafty forward Jordan Weal has taken off this season, becoming the first 17 year old in over a decade to reach 100 points in the WHL. That is more than WHL stars such as Eberle, Ryan Getzlaf, Tyler Ennis, or Peter Mueller were able to accomplish as 17 year olds.

At first glimpse, scouts are concerned about Weal's size. That said, his consistent production throughout the season is impossible to ignore and his high-end skills are certainly no fluke. In fact, his overall skill-set is in the high-end of the draft. His stick skills are dazzling in the offensive zone and help him to be a great playmaker. However, Weal has no problem sniping the puck. His versatility and creativity in the offensive zone makes Weal a threat every time he hits the ice. Moreover, Weal was able to shine against the toughest competition when playing in the CHL Top Prospects game.

PROJECTION

While his size was and remains a concern, Weal's consistent production has made him rise in the HockeyProspect.com rankings. Weal could certainly follow a similar pattern to Ennis (a Buffalo prospect) who we had ranked higher than most two years ago. Ennis, an undersized offensive dynamo had to take some time to adjust to the professional game, but looks to have stuck in Buffalo. Weal will need to get similarly comfortable as the size of the competition increases. Therefore, we see Weal as a late first or early second round pick (Ennis was selected 26th overall).

Brad Ross

Left Wing – Portland (WHL)
Born May 28 1992 -- Lethbridge, ALTA
Height 6.01 Weight 173 Shoots R

SCOUTING REPORT

Brad Ross is a solid prospect who has an NHL frame he can grow into. He has good speed and his first few steps are pretty good as well, especially for a bigger player. His hands and shot are solid as well.

He needs to bring up the consistency level as we are left wanting more on some shifts and some games. We have noticed an improvement in this regard lately though. Ross can be guilty of some unnecessary turnovers at times, mostly due to just over handling of the puck in high traffic. We love his speed and he does a great job of utilizing it, especially through the neutral zone, where he seems to be pressuring the opposing defenseman in the blink of an eye.

His play without the puck may be his biggest drawback, as he sometimes seems to lack the same passion and fire he plays with when he is involved on a rush or working the boards in the opponents end. He needs to be more conscious of his defensive responsibilities and have his head on a swivel a bit more often.

PROJECTION

We may sound like we are down on Ross because of the drawbacks in his game. The truth is his weaknesses are very easily fixable, so they might not hurt his stock as much as some would think. You can't teach the size, speed and playmaking abilities Ross is blessed with. We like him as an early to mid 2nd round selection and if he works on the minor flaws in his game and fills out his frame with muscle, he could very well be a steal in that area of the draft.

Alex Petrovic

Defense - Red Deer (WHL)
Born Mar 3 1992 Edmonton, ALTA
Height 6.04 Weight 193 Shoots R

SCOUTING REPORT

Alex Petrovic, a Red Deer defenseman, is one of just two gritty, tough, defensemen considered top 50 prospects in this draft (the second being Dylan McIlrath of Moose Jaw). Not surprisingly, it was Petrovic who took on McIlrath in a bout during the CHL top prospects game. In his second season for Red Deer, Petrovic saw a substantial increase in his stats, and became a much more valuable player for the squad.

Similar to McIlrath, Petrovic plays a tough, nasty, in your face game. He is always willing to ramp up the intensity and therefore wins tons of one on one battles. He also does a good job controlling the boards. His game is quite simple, bordering on predictable, so he could use some creativity in his play. That said, he has decent enough gap control. Where he runs into trouble sometimes is in defensive zone coverage. Essentially, Petrovic is a valuable one on one player, who will make forwards pay if they want to have a presence in the offensive zone. He needs to work on his defensive awareness, however.

In the offensive zone, Petrovic shows the ability to read the play well. He also has a good, right-handed shot from the point.

PROJECTION

Petrovic projects to be a steady defenseman in the NHL. He has not yet shown the ability to be a top-pairing player, but has the size and one on one capabilities to develop into a solid NHL defenseman. We don't see Petrovic as a first round talent, but should go in the first half of the second round.

Jared Knight

Center- London (OHL)
Born Jan 16 1992 Battle Creek, MI
Height 5.11 Weight 180 Shoots R

SCOUTING REPORT

Michigan born Jared Knight has spent the past two seasons with London of the Ontario Hockey League. He has come on strong since the beginning of the 2010 season, adding to an already much improved stat-sheet since his first year with London. After his diagnosis of Diabetes, Knight's game has really taken off.

Knight can play in all three zones but needs to be more consistent on his effort on the backcheck. We believe Knight could have easily played on London's first power play unit all year long. In terms of offensive production, Knight has a great shot. The puck seems to find him and he scores both accurate, goal scorer's goals and grinder, dirty area goals. When not showing off his shot, Knight shows no fear in crashing the net and heading into the offensive zone with authority. This grit element of his game is reminiscent of Canadian Olympian Mike Richards. London's record when he registers a point is 34-4-0-0. Their record when he is pointless is 11-11-1-2.

PROJECTION

We don't make a ton of NHL comparisons as we feel it's a bit unfair. In Knight's case when we see him uncork an accurate one-timer and find the quiet scoring areas of the ice, we some see flashes of Brett Hull.

It will be interesting to see when Knight gets snatched up in the draft. We see Knight as an early second rounder but he may not go that high. Knight could prove to be one of the steals of the 2010 draft. If he continues to develop, Knight can be a gritty, well-rounded forward with offensive punch in the NHL.

Joey Hishon

Center - Owen Sound (OHL)
Born Oct 20, 1991 Stratford, ONT
Height 5.10 Weight 190 Shoots L

SCOUTING REPORT

Joey Hishon recently completed his third OHL season with the Owen Sound Attack. Unfortunately, his season was a bit injury plagued, but he did show the standard over a point per game production like in his previous OHL campaigns. Hishon is a bit of an undersized center, but his stature should not be an issue going forward.

The first thing that sticks out about Hishon is his speed. He has great speed when he gets going and is quick to accelerate and explode. Moreover, he knows how to use his speed on the rush. He also has great puck skills that help him produce in the offensive zone. Still, while in the offensive zone, Hishon could stand to distribute the puck more often. Hishon always has shown great ability without the puck. He is solid on the penalty kill and in the defensive zone. Finally, despite not being huge, Hishon battles for the puck and plays an aggressive game.

PROJECTION

Even though Hishon showed a bit of rust in his game this season due to injuries, his draft status should not be hurt too greatly. With his skill-set, speed and mature game without the puck, Hishon could possibly be a late first round pick or an early 2nd rounder.

John McFarland

C/ Left Wing - Sudbury (OHL)
Born Apr 2 1992 Richmond Hill, ONT
Height 6.00 Weight 192 Shoots R

SCOUTING REPORT

Once projected to be a potential top 5 pick, John McFarland of the Sudbury Wolves just hasn't developed his game in a manner we would like to see. Still, McFarland is someone that shows flashes of a great player and this continues to make him a very tough prospect to project.

McFarland has terrific speed and the ability to blow by defenders, but too often he produces little off the rush. His shot was already NHL caliber power wise in Minor Midget. He had been deadly streaking down the ice as a sniper. It would seem that some of that accuracy is missing right now.

We would like to see more play-making and improved vision in his game to make him a more multi-faceted prospect. While he has shown signs of better play in his own zone, he will need to improve more. He has a great understanding of the game when you talk to him off the ice. We can't figure out why it doesn't translate onto the ice. He is the type of player with the skill set to put up more than a PPG and even dominate at this level, but his game has not yet matured enough mentally to reach that level.

PROJECTION

Whether or not he becomes an NHL player or not could lie in his own hands. If he shows a strong work ethic and desire to improve his overall game, he could realize his potential. A disappointing season based on his overall game has McFarland's draft status in question. Like many players his age, he is going to need to mature, but unlike many players his age, if McFarland matures and tackles his weaknesses, we think he can be an impact player in the NHL.

Kirill Kabanov

Left Wing – Moncton (QMJHL)
Born Jul 16 1992
Height 6.03 Weight 176 Shoots R

SCOUTING REPORT

Kirill Kabanov entered this season as almost a sure-fire top five if not top three pick. Long heralded as the next, dynamic Russian scoring forward, Kabanov made the move to the QMJHL in order to help himself realize his dream of entering the NHL. Unfortunately, he incurred a wrist injury, which has limited his playing time, and issues with Russia left him off the World Junior

Championship roster. Kabanov has not had much time to show just how talented he is.

Kabanov has as good, if not a better skill-set then just about anyone in the draft. There is nothing he can't accomplish with his stick or in the offensive zone. He has elite quickness and shiftiness that can render defenseman helpless. At the age of 17, he was already blowing away Canadian scouts. Kabanov has a great compete level, plays with an edge, and has made it clear his dream is to play in the NHL. The only thing he needs to improve on is his discipline. He is not a lazy player, but sometimes his edge and compete level gets the best of him in terms of taking too many penalties. He is also a bit lanky, but should be able to add muscle to his frame.

PROJECTION

G.M's will have the standard dilemma about drafting a Russian player with regards to Kabanov. Other Russian stars such Nikita Filatov and Alexander Radulov have both recently bolted to the KHL. Moreover, with the events towards the conclusion of his season (including leaving Moncton and then the U-18 Russian team), GM's will not be comfortable drafting Kabanov. His draft potential is a huge wild-card. He is a top ten talent, but with his off- ice issues, the freefall of his draft stock could be a long one.

Kevin Hayes

C/LW Noble & Greenough (HS- MA)
Born May 1992 Dorchester, Mass
Height 6.03 Weight 200 Shoots: L

SCOUTING REPORT

Hayes is a very good skater with a long, powerful stride. He is deceptively quick, his first couple of steps aren't great, but he has superb top-end speed and has the ability to change direction rapidly. He has outstanding edge control with strength and balance. He has nice lateral agility and is able to back defenders up or blow by them with speed and inside-outside moves through the neutral and offensive zones. Hayes is an excellent stickhandler who can advance the puck well in traffic. Hayes has very good size, and could grow an additional 1-2 inches and add 30 pounds when he physically matures; uses his bulk to shield the puck/ward off defenders. He is excellent on face-offs; uses strength/size to move opponent off of the puck and his quick enough hands to win draws outright. Big slap shot that he can uncork quickly on the fly. He sports a heavy, accurate wrist shot with pro-caliber release.

Kevin has good hockey sense, sees the ice well, but could use improvement in puck distribution.

He likes to take the puck behind the net and set up shop in similar fashion to Joe Thornton. Hayes won't always play a physical game though he doesn't shy away from contact either. He tends to stay out on the perimeter and doesn't always drop the shoulder and take the puck (and his man) to the net; sometimes content to take low percentage shots from the outside or throw it into the middle for a teammate.

Hayes is a good two-way player who shows a willingness to skate hard and hustle in the defensive zone. He plays a good offensive game that translates well at the prep level, but is not dominant by any stretch. There are still questions over whether he can do it at the next level. He needs to get stronger/fill out his big frame, but definitely has some upside. The high-end skill is clearly there, but he holds onto the puck too long at times looking for the perfect play. Hayes was named to the NEPSIHA East All-Star Team.

PROJECTION

Darkhorse 1st rounder - might just go ahead of Coyle because his size and skill level is better. Solid early to mid 2nd-round pick with the potential to be a top-six offensive center or winger.

Calvin Pickard

Goalie - Seattle (WHL)
Born Apr 15, 1992 Winnipeg, MAN
Height 6.01 Weight 208 Catches L

SCOUTING REPORT

Calvin Pickard, the brother of Nashville prospect Chet Pickard, is the top ranked goalie from the WHL to enter the draft this season. He has improved his game at a steady pace since his first season, and has turned into quite a formidable goaltender for the Seattle Thunderbirds, playing over 60 games!

He is a big player, at 6'1" 205 pounds, and plays

a "big goalie's game." He has quick reflexes, doesn't give up on a shot, and is good at playing the puck from behind the net. Although his movements may be considered slightly unorthodox, he has good lateral movement and moves quite well for a big kid. Fortunately, he is also a workhorse with a good mental make up for a goalie. He maintains great focus and is not rattled easily.

One thing we believe he needs to work on is his rebound control. As he plays at a higher level, shots are going to get more difficult and masked, so he needs to work on developing a strategy to limit second chances for the opponents.

PROJECTION

With goalies, a lot of where they are drafted has to do with team needs. Pickard should be the second goalie taken, behind the U.S. born Jack Campbell. We believe Calvin is a safe pick in early second round and could develop into a solid NHL goaltender.

Brooks Macek

Center – Tri City Americans (WHL)
Born May 15 1992 Winnipeg, MAN
Height 5.11 Weight 170 Shoots R

SCOUTING REPORT

Brooks Macek is a WHL center-man who most recently played for the Tri-City Americans. He put up absolutely monster numbers in Midget AAA (for Notre Dame) before joining the WHL, and since then has greatly improved his overall game. As his playing time increased this season, Macek showed more and more of what he could do.

Macek is a very good skater. He has top end speed, and is strong on his skates. He also uses his speed to crash the net hard and be physical. He also has a nice grit factor to his game. Macek certainly plays bigger than his 5'11" frame. He is a very skilled player, who has improved his hockey smarts greatly since beginning to play against more elite competition. He already had great vision, but has put it all together to look like a high-end playmaker recently. As the year progressed, he also improved his overall decision making on the ice.

Macek isn't quite where we would like on the defensive end of the ice. He needs to keep working on this two-way portion of the game. However, there is certainly marked improvement in this aspect of his game, which is a good sign for his future.

PROJECTION

Macek is a good prospect. He has some developing to do, but his steady improvement throughout the season is very promising. His high end playmaking ability, combined with improved overall play make him a viable second round pick with 2nd or 3rd line NHL potential.

Ryan Spooner

Center – Peterborough Petes (OHL)
Born Jan 30 1992 Kanata, ONT
Height 5.10 Weight 175 Shoots L

SCOUTING REPORT

Ryan Spooner is a small, speedy center for the Peterborough Petes of the OHL. Although he has seen a decrease in goals scored, Spooner still put up plenty of points in his OHL campaign and was selected as a member of the Canadian U-18 team.

Spooner is a great skater and is incredibly shifty on the ice; almost like a jitterbug out there beating opponents. His own coach raves about his one-on-one ability and dynamic impact on the ice. Specifically, Spooner has a combination of great speed and agility. Once in the offensive zone, Spooner has terrific vision that rivals that of top prospect Tyler Seguin. He also has a good nose for the net, and has the knack where pucks seem to find him.

What keeps Spooner out of the first round for HockeyProspect.com list, is a combination of his size and his play without the puck. He is going to need to get bigger to handle playing against professional players. Also, his work without the puck needs improvement and he needs to show more effort on the defensive end of the puck.

PROJECTION

Spooner's offensive talent and elite skating ability make for a promising NHL future. However, like one of his favorite players, Danny Briere, he is going to have to learn to use his skating to make an impact on all ends of the ice and get strong enough to compete in the NHL. The offensive skills will always be there though. We believe Spooner is a pretty solid selection from pick #40 onward in the draft.

Ivan Telegin

Center - Saginaw (OHL)
Born Feb 28, 1992 , Russia
Height 6.03 Weight 185 Shoots L

SCOUTING REPORT

Ivan Telegin, a big Russian winger, recently completed his first season with the Saginaw Spirit of the Ontario Hockey League. A lunch-pail player, Telegin didn't put up great numbers in the OHL, but proved himself to be a viable contributor in the league, nonetheless.

Telegin is the type of player that doesn't exactly excel at anything on the ice, but he certainly can contribute in all aspects of the game. He plays well against the wall and knows how to use his size in that aspect of the game, as well as to protect the puck. Moreover, like you would expect out of a player like Telegin, he goes to the net very hard and has no issue getting things done in the dirty areas of the ice. Therefore, he is the guy for Saginaw that will score the ugly goals when the pretty ones aren't coming. However, his puck skills are just decent, and he does not seem to be able to have an explosive offensive impact.

PROJECTION

Telegin is a nice prospect for sure. You have to appreciate what he does on the ice and how he has fallen into a nice role on his team. That same role needs to be filled on most NHL teams as well. That said, with his skill-set, he doesn't look to be a top line scorer in the NHL. Therefore, he will likely be a second round pick in the draft.

Charlie Coyle

Right Wing - South Shore (EJHL)
Born March 2nd 1992 Weymouth, MA
Height: 6.02 Weight 202 Shoots R

SCOUTING REPORT

Coyle is a player possessing a big frame, with more room to fill out. He's a good skater with solid east-west agility and mobility. Coyle has a long, powerful stride. His first step needs improvement, but top speed is fine.

Coyle is a good stickhandler who can take the puck effectively into traffic and maintain control. He protects the puck very well down low, along the boards and on the cycle. He is not afraid to go hard to the net and has an accurate, hard shot. Charlie fights hard for loose pucks along the walls and wins most of the 1-on-1 battles.

Used on the point of the power play he reads plays well and has good positioning to keep the puck in along the blue line. He uses a low, hard snapshot that he gets off quickly.

He plays a physical, banging style to go with a skilled offensive game. Coyle doesn't try to go out of his way for the big open ice hit, but will initiate contact as well as take the hit to make the play. He has a good compete level and will back check and pick up his man. Coyle has NHL bloodlines,. He is the cousin of Tony Amonte. Charlie is committed to BU for the fall of 2010.

PROJECTION

Solid 2nd round selection- probably one of the 1st 15 picks in that round, and shouldn't drop past the 50th pick in the draft. Good upside as a top-six forward and PP specialist. Coyle is versatile and intelligent with prototypical size NHL teams like. He should continue to add strength and develop; versatile, well-rounded player who has benefited from the 60+ game pro-style schedule in the 'E' this year

Petr Straka

LW - Rimouski (QMJHL)
Born Jun 15 1992, Czech
Height 6.01 Weight 180 Shoots L

SCOUTING REPORT

Petr Straka, a Czech born winger, recently completed his season for Rimouski of the QMJHL. He proved himself to be a point per game player at the Major Junior level. Straka had an opportunity to play for Team Orr at the CHL Top Prospects game. Straka has the size to be an NHL forward.

Straka's draft status is based almost purely on his offensive prowess. Dominant in the Czech Republic before jumping to North America, Straka's offensive game translated well. Skating-wise, he has good speed and has good balance, despite not being the prettiest skater on the ice. He has a nice skill set, with soft hands and the ability to take good quality shots on net. He also isn't afraid to go to the dirty areas in the offensive zone. Overall, he just has great scoring instincts. He reads the play very well in the offensive zone, making him equally adept at both playmaking and scoring.

Unfortunately, Straka's offensive vision hasn't translated to the defensive end. He doesn't read the play well in the defensive zone and really needs to learn how to compete on every shift, regardless of where the puck is on the ice. However, he has shown the propensity to be a solid penalty killer.

PROJECTION

Straka is arguably a first round offensive talent. However, he has much to learn about the other areas of the ice and competing, which should land him in the second round. If he improves more in the defensive zone, Straka could be a solid draft choice and become a scoring forward in the NHL.

Troy Rutkowski

Defense – Portland (WHL)
Born Apr 29 1992 Edmonton, ALTA
Height 6.01 Weight 219 Shoots R

SCOUTING REPORT

Troy Rutkowski, a defenseman for Portland of the WHL is quite an impressive offensive talent on the back end. He is quite strong and has a good offensive skill-set. He has increased his production greatly in his second season in the WHL and with the coaching he gets in Portland, should have great opportunity to round out his game.

Rutkowski can be considered the type of player that has many of the tools, but has to put it all together if he wants to progress to the next level. He has shown the ability, which is evident by his numbers, to control the game from the back-end in the offensive zone. He also has the capability to quarterback the power play at an elite level and can be a physical presence.

What it comes down to with Rutkowski is harnessing these various skills into a complete package. He is the type of player that has shown glimpses all season of being an easy first round talent, but consistency is a question mark. He needs to be more physical and work on his decision-making in the defensive end, as well when to join the rush.

PROJECTION

Rutkowski is a classic high-risk/high-reward player. He has shown glimpses of being a well rounded, two-way impact defenseman. However, he does have some holes in his game that he needs to work out. His upside makes Rutkowski a top 50 talent in our books.

Curtis Hamilton

Left Wing – Saskatoon (WHL)
Born Dec 4 1991 Kelowna, BC
Height 6.03 Weight 202 Shoots L

SCOUTING REPORT

Hamilton is the son of Bruce Hamilton, a former Blades forward and current Owner and General Manager of the Kelowna Rockets. Hamilton was selected by the Blades in the 2nd round (36th overall) in the 2006 Bantam Draft He plays a good two way game, has come miles in this area as he was just a pure offence guy when he entered the league. Curtis was also a member of Team

Canada at the 2009 World Under-18 Hockey Championship in Fargo, ND.

Hamilton plays a smart game without the puck and does a good job of being where he is supposed to be in his own zone. His stick is pretty active and he does a decent job of getting it into lanes.

On offence he sees the ice well and does a good job distributing the puck. Hamilton also does a really good job in the transition game. His vision and smart play leads to really good decisions as he moves the puck up ice. He does a solid job of moving up ice with the play and gaining the zone. This allows him to become an important part of the offence on rushes.

PROJECTION

Injuries have made him a tougher prospect to get a grasp on this season, but we see him as player with good potential because of his improved overall game. A late 2nd rounder seems about where he might fit into this draft.

Andrew Yogan

Center - Erie Otters (OHL)
Born Dec 4 1991 Boca Raton, FL
Height 6.03 Weight 202 Shoots L

SCOUTING REPORT

Yogan is a big kid who has flown under the radar a little bit in his career. Yogan was behind some of the big guns with the Spitfires and was dealt to Erie where he has seen more ice time and was given an opportunity to try to showcase himself.

Yogan is strong on the walls and does a good job protecting the puck. He plays a pretty smart game when he wants to. He has an outstanding shot that he can get off quickly in traffic. He is not a player with any real weakness in the skills department. He is probably not an elite player in any one facet of the game though.

The biggest knock on Yogan for us is that he takes too many shifts off. There are times when he flat out looks lazy out on the ice. There is zero room for players with his current level of work ethic in the NHL. He has shifts where he fails to backcheck, and shifts where he does not look very interested in playing defense in his own zone.

PROJECTION

We love his long reach and scoring ability. At 6'3" and tipping the scale at over 200 pounds, Yogan is a player with NHL size. He has improved his game each year in the league. Yogan needs to work on improving his quickness and his consistency. We love smart hockey players and Yogan is in that category. There is always a market for huge players like Yogan. He can put the puck in the net and work the puck down low.

Yogan will probably decide his own destiny as far as his hockey career goes. We really like a lot about his game. In the end, you can have a boat load of talent but you also need a good solid work ethic to go along with it. We see him as a 2nd rounder just on the talent and size alone.

Ryan Martindale

Center - Ottawa (OHL)
Born Oct 27, 1991 Brooklin, ONT
Height 6.03 Weight 182 Shoots L

SCOUTING REPORT

Ryan Martindale is a big-bodied center who recently played his third season with the Ottawa 67's of the Ontario Hockey League. He has shown a steady increase in production each season, as he has developed into Ottawa's first line center.

Beyond being a big player, Martindale has soft hands and extra-ordinary playmaking ability. He plays a smart game and has quick shot that he can easily get off in high traffic areas. He also has a nice shot off the rush. He has a great frame for the NHL and should be able to add some muscle. He has also added some aggression into his game which is a must for players his size. He needs to play up to his size more often and get involved more along the walls.

That said, he needs to show more urgency on a shift-by-shift basis. Still, he does work hard enough in the defensive zone and plays a smart game on that end of the ice. Martindale's biggest drawback might be his skating. He is going to have to improve in that area if he wants to play in the NHL. His shot is good, but needs to develop even more to be productive at the NHL level as a goal scorer.

PROJECTION

With his size and offensive ability, Martindale should attract serious NHL attention come draft day. However, like many big players, his ability to use his size against NHL players, along with an improvement in skating will be the key to his game translating. Martindale could go in the first round, but we see him down the rankings a bit based on his current compete level. We like to see less of a perimeter game from him.

Sam Brittain

Goalie – Canmore (AJHL)
Born May 10 1992 Calgary, ALTA
Height 6.03 Weight 215 Catches L

SCOUTING REPORT

Brittain led the Calgary Buffaloes AAA Midget team to the Telus Cup in Selkirk, Manitoba, last spring, winning a silver medal. Brittain is a huge goalie and he moves very well, covering a ton of net. He has had a strong season in Canmore and has landed an NCAA ride to Denver.

Brittain won't blow you away with his GAA numbers, as he faces plenty of shots on most nights playing for an average team. That makes it next to impossible to post numbers matching goalies from some of the stronger teams. He did post a 91.25% save percentage in the playoffs which is impressive.

We would classify Sam as a butterfly goaltender who plays a smart game. He knows his angles and his positioning is very strong. Brittain does a good job of reading the play and makes great adjustments to the shooter. He gets square to the shooter more often than not.

PROJECTION

His draft stock might drop for some NHL teams depending on their views on the quality of shooters in the AJHL. There is no question on Brittain's ability to stop the puck. He is very solid technically and is very quick for a big kid. We are high on Sam and rank him as the 3rd best goalie in the draft. We rank him as a late second rounder.

Yasin Cisse

Forward - Des Moines (USHL)
Born Mar 11 1992 Westmount, PQ
Height 6.03 Weight 208 Shoots R

A season ending ankle injury put an end to a very fast start for Yasin. Cisse had 13 goals in just 19 games when he went down to injury.

Cisse has elite skills, is 6'3" and weighs in at 208 lbs. His shot, release and scoring skills are very good. His play without the puck is also quite good. In general there is not much to dislike about this player. The only thing that we consider a weakness, is a bit of an ugly stride. This keeps him from being a high end skater. He does not look slow, it's more of agility skating and the first few steps. He played with some real sandpaper in Midget AAA with the Lac St. Louis Lions and we expect that to return to his game once he gets his feet wet at a higher level.

He has scoring skills, is an above average playmaker, and he was a proven gritty player in the past. We can't wait to see what round he is drafted in. This player has caused some really interesting arguments amongst some of our staff. The injury scared off some of our guys, but in the end we still like him in round two.

Stephen Silas

Defense - Belleville (OHL)
Born Jun 26 1992 Georgetown, ONT
Height 6.00 Weight 190 Shoots L

We liked him with the Halton Hurricanes and he has done little to change our opinion since his OHL career began. He is a very strong player in multiple facets of the game. Silas does not panic with the puck. Show me a d-man who panics and I'll show you a d-man with a rough career ahead. Silas stays cool and collected and makes good reads coming out of his own zone. Passes are on the tape and accurate.

He can play a physical game as well as a great positional game, using his stick to perfection. He understands defense and the importance of positional play and stick position.

He is capable of carrying the puck up ice and mixes in head fakes to open lanes or passing options. He has put up points and has a great head for the offensive side of the game. Don't let the points fool you though. This kid can play a pretty solid shutdown game as well. If Silas was slightly bigger, he would most likely be talked about with some of the big names. 6'0" is not small but in today's NHL, 6'0 defenseman need to possess a solid skill set on their resume. We are obviously high on Silas and would not be shocked to see him snatched up earlier than many think.

Brian Billett

Goalie - Jr. Monarchs (EJHL)
March 19 1992 - Kennebunk, Maine
Height 6-1 Weight 185 Catches: Left

Billett has good height and is long-limbed with excellent reflexes and quickness. He needs to add weight to his frame, but has a lean athletic body. Billett has a weird stance; lower-than-normal crouch, which reduces his upper coverage of the net. He has extremely quick legs; down-to-up movement and recovery is outstanding. His lateral post-to-post movement is very good. Billett has a quick glove, but needs to get better at catching the puck cleanly. He has solid positioning…doesn't overplay the shot and stays square to the shooter. He rolled his ankle this summer and struggled in the early portion of the season trying to come back too soon. He's mentally tough and focused: plays on an a team that doesn't give up a lot of shots, which can be more taxing than playing on a poor defensive team that gives up a lot of scoring chances. He can see long stretches of inactivity, followed by a flurry of quality scoring chances and odd-man rushes. He holds up well under that kind of pressure.

Brian is highly intelligent and dedicated to improving his game. He places heavy emphasis on preparation and is a respected leader in the room even though he is a quiet presence who goes out and does his job without theatrics. Billett is very calm and poised. He is relaxed…almost Martin Brodeur-like in terms of being able to shrug off pre-game pressure and butterflies to focus and play at a high level when the puck is dropped.

He is underrated. His numbers have been tremendous in his second season after leading NH Monarchs to a national Jr. 'A' championship last year. Billett stopped 90 of 93 shots in the final three games to close out the regular season.

Billett is a dark-horse candidate for a team picking around 55-60 that isn't afraid of EJHL competition and likes a big-game player with upside. We expect that he is more likely to be a mid 3rd-round or solid 4th-rounder, but nowhere near Central Scouting's 25th ranking among N.A. goalies - that's garbage.

Billett has NHL potential as a starter, but will require time and patience. We love this kid. If we were an NHL staff, we would start pounding the table late the 2nd Round to grab him.

Jerome Gauthier-Leduc
Defense - Rouyn-Noranda (QMJHL)
Born Jul 30 1992 Quebec, PQ
Height 6.01 Weight 171 Shoots R

Leduc is a very smooth skater with good lateral mobility and quick feet. His mobility makes him pretty solid off the rush. He can get 'ugly' at times when he tries to do too much with the puck. Like many young players his play without the puck is suspect at times. The numbers he has posted speak volumes about his offensive upside. He is a right shot defenseman with a very hard wrist shot that he gets through.

Sam Carrick

Center - Brampton (OHL)
Born Feb 4 1992 Stouffville, ONT
Height 6.00 Weight 188 Shoots R

Carrick might be a steal for some team is he falls to a later round. He plays in the ultra conservative Stan Butler scheme and played alongside a group of very young forwards in Brampton. Carrick is not huge, but has enough size to play in the NHL. He is a strong kid and uses his size well when he battles for pucks. He does a good job down low on the walls and makes good decisions with the puck.

We love the way he drives the net and protects the puck off the rush. He plays with a little sandpaper in his game and we don't think he gets enough credit for his offensive skills.

Carrick suffered an injury during the playoffs and it was very clear that his absence hurt the Brampton Battalion.

Playing for Butler has driven home how to play the game without the puck, which is a real asset for him when he goes pro. Don't be surprised if this kid puts up some pretty good numbers in the OHL before his time in the league is done.

Kent Simpson

Goalie - Everett (WHL)
Born Mar 26 1992 Edmonton, ALTA
Height 6.01 Weight 183 Catches L

We really like Simpson and he has made himself easy to appreciate this season. Kent has good size and makes himself look big in the net with solid positional play and mechanics. He has played alongside 1990 goaltender Thomas Heemskerk who signed a free agent deal with San Jose back in September. Simpson has carried the ball well in his starts posting a .925 save % and a 22-9-1 record. Kent is one of our higher rated goalies.

Mark Visentin

Goalie - Niagara (OHL)
Born Aug 7 1992 Waterdown, ONT
Height 6.00 Weight 176 Catches L

We can tell you from experience that Visentin is dedicated and has a great work ethic. We know this because Hockey Prospects founder helped out at a couple practices in Visentin's rookie year. Visentin has a great head on his shoulders and works hard on and off the ice to get better. He shared a billet with Alex Pietrangelo as a rookie, which probably helped him in his rookie season.

Mark Visentin was probably one of the most improved players in the OHL this season. The staff at HP would be stretching the truth if we told you that we knew all along how much he would improve. Looking back on it now, maybe it's not that surprising. Mark has the size, he moves very well from post to post, he's very quick and does a pretty good job challenging the shooters.

In his rookie year his trapper was not very good at all and Mark just let in too many soft goals. His rebound control was iffy at best, but he was a rookie tender playing a bunch of minutes with a rookie partner (John Cullen). We think that the trade for Jeremy Smith that took away his minutes was the best thing that could have happened to him. Visentin has said himself that he learned a ton from the vet.

This season he has played with a group of young defensemen in front of him. He is clearly bigger and stronger. He seems like a different player mentally, and his glove hand that made us wince at times last season is much improved. The only part of his game that might still need some improvement is his rebound control.

We think Visentin is a solid pickup as a late 2nd rounder. If he continues to improve at the same rate as he did this season, the sky is the limit for this goalie.

Jakub Culek

Center - Rimouski (QMJHL)
Born Sep 7 1992
Height 6.04 Weight 195 Shoots L

A huge kid at 6'4" 195 that will draw plenty of attention by NHL teams when you add the potential based on his skills. Culek comes into this draft just under the wire with a Sept 7th birth date. If he was born a bit later he would surely go as a higher pick next year. Jakub tests scouts ability to project, as he seems to have more potential than we see produced right now. Culek has us wanting and expecting more on too many nights. He will hold a solid spot in the draft based more on potential than what we have seen from him to date.

Teemu Pulkkinen

RW - Jokerit (SM-Liiga)
Born Jan 2 1992 Vantaa, Finland
Height 5.11 Weight 176 Shoots R

We love his hockey smarts and he seems to think the game at a high level. He also makes good reads in the offensive zone. It's been tough to get a good long look at him this season but we had pretty good viewings in the past. It would be nice to see him play for Finland this spring. Teemu can really shoot the puck and sports a deceptive release that seems to catch goalies off guard. His weakness would be his play without the puck in his own zone. We would love to see what he could do if he was playing in the CHL.

Injuries have been a huge factor in his declining stock of late. There is no question that he is a talented prospect but you can't blame any NHL team if the injuries scare them off a bit. We still like him as a 3rd rounder and he could be a steal at that spot if he can shake the constant injury bug.

Louis-Marc Aubry

Center - Montreal (QMJHL)
Born Nov 11, 1991
Height 6.02 Weight 181 Shoots L

Louis-Marc Aubry of the Montreal Juniors is a talented two-way center. He has great size, with plenty of room to add some muscle. He has taken on the role as one of the top, defensive centers in the CHL, modeling his game after Jordan Staal of the Pittsburgh Penguins. That said, he has shown offensive improvement from his first QMJHL campaign to his second one.

Aubry is a high-end center in terms of his defensive play. He has a long reach that he uses well and also uses his body well as an imposing figure on the ice. He always finishes his checks and works hard to win battles in the defensive zone. He plays a mature game, is very coachable and does little things on the ice that most players his age don't. He is the type of player that every successful team needs.

Despite his two-way prowess, Aubry could stand to improve his offensive game. We believe he is an under-rated playmaker, but he needs to develop some finish to make him a more well-rounded player.. The good thing is he isn't afraid of the dirty areas of the ice and loves to battle for the puck.

There is no doubt that he has the hockey sense, size and compete level to be a solid defensive center. Depending on his offensive production, his upside is a big center that is polished in all aspects of the game. His lack of current offensive numbers should leave him out of the top rounds.

Martin Ouellette

Goalie - Kimball Union Academy (HS)
Born December 30, 1991
Height 6.01 Weight 160 Catches Left

Ouellette is a prototypical NHL goaltender in terms of size, athleticism and ability to play a fundamentally-sound butterfly style. He has big presence who takes up a lot of the net. He plays with a compact stance, is smooth with an economy of motion on every save. He does not get scrambly or lose body position on the shot. He is aggressive and challenges the shooter. He has the best glove hand of any goalie seen this year in New England. He catches every puck cleanly that goes anywhere near his glove.

Ouellette has very good rebound control. He plays even better under pressure; calm, unflappable, and in control of his emotions. He gave up three goals in two games we watched in the playoff tourney: all deflections that he had no chance on. If he sees it, he stops it. He needs to add weight to his skinny frame. He has potential to lose focus at times and give up the odd soft goal. Only real knock on him is level of competition, but he dominated at KUA.

Danny Biega

Defense - Harvard University (ECAC)
Born Sep 29 1991 Montreal, PQ
Height 6.00 Weight 200 Shoots R

Biega is an average skater with ok first-step quickness, average straight-line speed, but very good agility and pivoting/turning ability. He is undersized and struggles with containing bigger, stronger forwards who go hard to the net. He's not afraid to take the body and initiate contact along the boards though. He will need to rely on quickness and positioning/angling to be effective at the next level.

Danny sees the ice extremely well and has the natural instincts to effectively retrieve the puck in his own end and move it out of the zone quickly. He makes a crisp first pass; an effective puck mover with good recovery speed. Biega likes to take the body and is a smart hitter given his disadvantage against bigger, stronger players. He was an outstanding two-way defender in the prep championships last spring. As captain he led Salisbury School to the championship with cool, calm poise in his own end and aggressive play in the offensive zone. Biega is a very good point man that keeps the puck in along the blue line and generates surprising power on his shot given his size. His skating for a small guy is a bit of a concern. It's not a detriment, but in context of his lack of size, probably drops him in the rankings a bit. He has yet to assert himself at Harvard in his true freshman year, but is progressing nicely in the second half; showing confidence and upside.

Bill Arnold
Forward - USA NTDP (USHL)
Born May 13 1992 Needham, MA
Height 5.11 Weight 185 Shoots R

Arnold is an above average skater with decent change of direction; short and squat - built like a fire hydrant and has a low center of gravity that makes him tough to knock off the puck. Quick hands and stick; when playing with confidence will go hard to the net and make things happen. Hard shot with quick release. Very good snap shot that he gets off well in traffic. Very effective in the corners where he uses leverage to fight off opponents and protect the puck.

Connor Brickley
Left Wing - Des Moines (USHL)
Born Feb 25 1992 Everett, MA
Height 6.02 Weight 195 Shoots L

Brickley is a solid skater; strong on his skates with a non-stop motor and very good speed. Above average puck skills who works hard in all zones. Plays a high-energy style; gets more out of his modest ability because of desire/heart. He is an aggressive forechecker who forces turnovers with a quick stick and anticipation. High hockey IQ; reads the developing play well and compensates for lack of elite skills by being in right place at right time. Connor scores opportunistic goals at big moments, even if he's not a constant productive presence. Brickley is a character player; does everything asked of him and more. Left Belmont Hill for the USHL, which is better for his development and provides a pro-style schedule in terms of games played and travel.

Pat McNally

Defense - Milton Academy (HS- MA)
Born December 4, 1991, Glen Head, NY
Height 6.02 Weight 180

Pat is a very good forward skater, with good first-step quickness and speed. Backward skating needs a lot of work: stiff, unbalanced and has trouble crossing over and squaring up to opponents who come at him with speed and lateral moves. He can be an undisciplined player who likes to gamble; rushes the puck with abandon and gets caught out of position. He sports superb on-ice vision and very good at puck distribution. He really makes a nice first pass coming out of the zone.

McNally is an effective triggerman on the power play with a big, heavy shot. Takes time to get it off with a big windup, though. Nice wrist shot that he can snap off quickly on the fly – very accurate. Shows a willingness to take the body, but lacks upper body power and strength. Defensive awareness and positioning needs a lot of work; hockey sense is a big question mark at this point. McNally Led all Milton players in scoring with 14 goals, 35 points in 28 games. He was named to the NEPSIHA East All-Star Team.

Michael Pereira
Left Wing - Avon Old Farms (HS- CT)

Pereira has average size, lean build that has a lot of filling out to do. He is an excellent skater with an explosive initial burst and extra separation gear. Dynamic offensive player who stepped up his game when it mattered most: in the prep playoffs, registering 3 goals, 3 assists in final two games en route to Avon's 8th prep title in 29 years. Quick stick; can make moves at top speed and not afraid to go into traffic. Creative playmaker with a real nose for the net; puck seems to follow him around the ice. Good release and accurate shot; goes into the slot and willing to take the hit to make the play. Pereira is an under-rated passer with soft hands and on-ice vision to find the open man. Beat NMH's fast and skilled forward Austin Cangelosi with speed to the outside before feeding a backhand pass to Quinn Smith for a short-handed goal in championship game. Mike is an average player defensively. Uneven season; doesn't always compete with the kind of energy and production he brought in the playoffs. Not a physical presence. Rough and raw; will likely need four years in college to mature physically and hone his overall game. Mike was named to the NEPSIHA West All-Star Team.

Mike Reardon
Defense Noble & Greenough (HS-MA)

Reardon is an excellent athlete and a multi-sport athlete who has focused on hockey, after being a standout in baseball and football. Above average skater; looks faster than he is because he has a high level of hockey sense. First step is an issue...has trouble getting to loose pucks when teams are cycling effectively. Makes a crisp first pass and sees the ice well. He's productive in prep, but looks more like a stay-at-home D at the next level. Good intangibles; works hard, a leader and sets a good example. Physical player who will give and take hits to make the play.

Nick Trecapelli
Defense – Sudbury Wolves (OHL)

Trecapelli has seen his OHL career take off since a mid season trade that sent him from Saginaw to Sudbury. The 6'0 d-man has seen his minutes increase from about 10 minutes per game with Saginaw to about 25 per game with the Wolves. Nick has great raw tools and just needs to play physical more consistently. Nick has pretty good feet and shows some agility for a big player. He is developing his game in the offensive end of the ice and is showing improvement. We would love to see him bring some real nastiness to his game. If he continues to improve at the same rapid rate since the trade up north, he could very well be a valuable pickup for some NHL team.

Andrew Shaw
Center – Niagara (OHL)

We ranked Shaw last season and still like him as a late round pickup. Shaw is a gamer and would seem to have the tools and makeup to find his way to a pro roster someday. We think if he is given a chance to play with some more offensive forwards, he will show off his under-rated scoring talent. The 1991 born Shaw is fearless and has dropped the gloves with players who have outweighed him by as much as 70 pounds and had over 3 inches on him. He may be a player that takes the long route to the NHL. You can't teach heart and this kid has tons of it.

Matt Petgrave
Defense - Niagara (OHL)

We have watched Petgrave up close the last three seasons. He has outstanding raw tools and a gives himself extra time and space with effective head fakes and escapabilty. He loves the offensive part of the game and is very gifted at joining the rush and playmaking. He gets his shot through from the point. Petgrave just needs to learn that it's not always the right time to rush the puck. He earned more ice time as each month passed this season. We think Petgrave has good upside and we think he is worth a pick at the end of the draft.

Colby Drost
Goalie - Holderness School (Prep)

We first saw Drost in a prospects event and were really impressed by how quickly he moved for a big kid. When we saw him last year the one knock on him was that he needed to drop some baby fat. His fitness plan this season dropped over 15 pounds and he is now listed at 6'1" 195 lbs.

Drost has played this season for a fairly weak prep school, after falling ill at an OHL main camp last fall. It was not uncommon for him to face 50 plus shots per game this year. His stats were solid and his mechanics are much improved this season. Coaches have raved about his work ethic.

Andrew Crescenzi
Center/Wing - Kitchener OHL

Can you say sleeper? Andrew is a big boy who has developed nicely this season. He was a very late bloomer hockey wise. The knock on him was always that he was a gentle giant. Andrew has room to improve still, but he has taken huge strides in his physical game with his 6'4" 210 pound frame. His skating is quite good for a big guy. When he gets rolling he is capable of beating defenders wide with speed and power. He does plenty of little things well and seems to have soaked up a quality coaching staffs teachings. If Andrew can fully transform himself into a very physical player next season, he will become a truly valuable player and prospect.

Mike MacDonald

Center - London Knights (OHL)

What an impressive stretch of scoring this past season. MacDonald popped in 21 of his 25 goals after an increase in ice time from December 1st through the end of the season. MacDonald scored the 21 goals in 32 games. Mike arrived to the Knights later than he planned. He had previously decided to go the NCAA route but changed his mind and headed to the OHL and the Knights.

Mike has great speed and very under-rated skills with the puck. He has come miles this season as far as developing his play without the puck. The Knights have surprised some people this season and players like MacDonald are the reason why.

Geoffrey Schemitsch
Defense - Owen Sound (OHL)

Geoffrey Schemitsch is an interesting story. He was all set to play for a friend of HP in Tier II Junior 'A' after being recruited out of Midget AAA. Schemitsch made the trip to Owen Sound for their main camp in late August and never returned to the Vaughan Vipers where he had planned to play this season.

Schemitsch has great offensive instincts and proved that very early on in his OHL career. He posted big numbers as a rookie d-man in the league. If he has a weakness it's that he shows his inexperience in his own zone while in defensive coverage.

Schemitsch is a strong skater with great mobility and he is strong playing one on ones off the rush. His puck movement skills are excellent and while his shot is not spectacular, it's not a weakness either. He can make the odd bad decision when pressured but when you factor in that he is a rookie who came out of nowhere, it's not a huge concern. He is gaining valuable experience in the league and should be ready for a nice second season. Some may say that we are reaching, but we like him as late 2nd or early 3rd rounder.

Johan Alm

Defense - Frolunda (Sweden Jr.)

Alm is a stay at home defenseman with really good size. At 6'2" the young defenseman has good strength and he plays a smart game in his own zone. It would seem that he won't develop into a points guy, so he will needs to continue to produce being a solid stay at home guy. He sometimes breaks down in coverage in his own end and loses his man.

We like Alm's upside but his feet will need to be quicker to progress as a true prospect. We think we might be reaching if we placed him any higher than the 3rd round.

Calle Jarnkrok
Center - Brynas (Sweden Jr.)

Calle is a good hockey player but at 5'11" 156 pounds he will need to pack on some weight to have any impact at the NHL level. His ceiling is high, as he is a very skilled player. Calle is a player with great hockey sense and vision on the ice. He has been better recently as Brynas entered the playoffs.

Jarnkrok is a tough one to rank as far as draft stock goes. He shows flashes of brilliance but can also go cold for long stretches. Size is a concern.

Julian Melchiori
Defense - Newmarket (CCHL)

Melchiori had a great season at Midget AAA with the Toronto Marlies and then moved on to Tier II and the Newmarket Hurricanes. He had a great rookie season and has followed it up with another fine season this year. The 14th round pick of the Oshawa Generals could have gone the OHL route but chose to accept a ride to UMass Lowell.

The 6'3" 195 pound defenseman does a good job of keeping it simple in his own zone. He makes a good first pass and can lug the puck himself as well.

Melchiori has great feet, quickness and acceleration. In fact his skating is just plain fantastic all around. This makes him an intriguing prospect given the huge frame he has a chance to grow into. He is a real chore to beat one on one and has good offensive skills to build on, as they are still a bit rough around the edges.

There is some pretty good upside for a team willing to forget about how depleted the talent was in this league in 2009/2010.

Nikita Zatsev
Defense - Sibir Novosibirsk

A defensive defenseman with a good break out pass, he needs to gain more confidence. He is a good junior player, but he needs to gain more experience playing against men as he still feels some pressure there. He does make a very good break out pass that can send the forwards through the neutral zone. He sees and reads the ice very well.

He tries hard to play tough along the boards, but he lacks some size and some confidence as he still tries to poke check instead of using the body. To play at the next level he also needs to be more creative with the puck and not just simply play it along the boards trying to avoid errors. Zatsev has good skating abilities although he'll seldom jump into rushes.

His strengths: good upside, good breakout pass and decent defensive play. Weaknesses would be lacking some strength and some creativity in the offensive zone. He also needs to work on his shot.

Nikita Gusev
RW - CSKA-Red Army

Gusev is a smallish winger with speed to burn and great skills. He can dangle very effectively in the offensive zone to take advantage over the opposition and likes making things happen with his moves. He has the ability to score beautiful breakaway goals and is lethal when the defenseman finds a stretch pass through the neutral zone to send him in alone on goal.

He has excellent puck handling skills. He doesn't like playing defense and is passive in his own end. His strengths are great speed, stick-handling and he just flat out knows how to score. His weaknesses are lack of size at 5'9" 155 pounds and his overall defensive play is just not good.

Sergei Barbashev
LW/RW - CSKA-Red Army

A good playmaking winger, Barbashev blends great skating with very good technique, opportunistic play and hard work.. He has great wheels and works very hard to get back in the zone to play defense but still struggles with D zone coverage. He doesn't always play physical enough and tries to stay on the perimeter too often. He uses his speed to get out of trouble when he is in high traffic situations. He has a very good touch around the net thanks to his quick wrist shot. He is a smart player with great speed. Size is an issue.

Alexei Marchenko
Defense - CSKA Moscow

Marchenko is the top 1992 defenseman from Russia. He is a complete defenseman who can play in any situation and has a knack for carrying the puck while skating with his head up. He has excellent skating mechanics and very good stickhandling skills. He's excellent reading the ice and can really pass the puck. Marchenko is not only an offensive player. He can be a very strong shutdown guy who is good in defensive coverage with some grit and aggression. You can add to the mix a lot of discipline as he rarely makes trips to the penalty box. He has solid NHL potential, but he will need to work on his shot.

Ignat Zemchenko
C/W - Almaz

Ignat is a player who can play all offensive positions. Zemchenko has a good nose for the net, but isn't ready yet for the more demanding North American physical game. If he wants to carry on playing center he has to work on his faceoff abilities. He has some value thanks to his versatility, but has to work harder on defense.

Artem Voronin
Center - Spartak Moscow

Voronin is an interesting playmaking center with very good playmaking abilities. He can bring the puck up through the neutral zone in style thanks to his very good stick handling. He's a bit of a streaky player. He can score two goals and three assists in a game and nothing in the next two.

His skating abilities are very good as well. He can score, but he is mostly a playmaker and just like many Russians prefers passing over shooting. He usually tries to stay away from trouble and from overly physical play.

His strengths are creative playmaking. His weakness would be a lack of physical play.

Alex Micallef
Defense – Villanova (OJAHL)

Alex was recruited to Villanova out of Junior B where he was a teammate of Trevor Parkes (now with the Montreal Juniors) Alex had an outstanding year and improved throughout the whole season. Alex played a very tight gap all over the ice and was very physical.

Micallef is tough as nails and although he does not think of himself as a fighter, he knew when he needed to drop the gloves and destroyed almost every opponent. Alex put up big points with good vision and passing accuracy on the power play.

Micallef is 6'0 200 pounds and is built like a rock. Not only is he very skilled but he is also willing to support his teammates. We saw him fight on two occasions and he can really throw punches. He had several NCAA schools including Niagara taking a serious look at him. He returned home to Fort Erie after Christmas for school reasons. It killed the finish to his season.

Alex's skating is good. He needs to get a bit quicker handling outside speed as he occasionally pivots a bit late. We noticed improvement late in the season.

His work on the power play was impressive. He did a great job reading the ice and hit seams on a regular basis. His passes are crisp and accurate. He is pretty good at getting to the middle of the ice and get is shot through traffic.

We won't be surprised to see Alex get a chance to play at a higher level and showcase his skills to more scouts. When he shows his smarts on the ice combined with that toughness and strength it should put him on the map.

Tommy O'Regan
Center - St. Sebastian's (HIGH- MA)

Tommy is a decent skater with a nice blend of size and speed with some giddy-up (initial burst). He is a good stickhandler who handles the biscuit with confidence and makes his moves at top speed.

O'Regan is tall and lanky, but plays a jitterbug style with slick moves, head fakes and rapid crossovers/change in direction. His footwork has improved from last season, but still needs improvement to be effective at the next level.

Tommy has a quick shot that is hard and accurate. He has a really nice backhand that he's not afraid to use. O'Regan can be a bit of a one-man show at times and needs to work on his puck distribution/using teammates more effectively, but he can put the puck in in the net.

2

PLAYER INTERVIEWS
(Transcriptions)

Erik Gudbranson
Defense – Kingston Frontenacs
Released on 13 December 2009

HP: Erik, you're certainly off to a strong start this season. What's been going well for you personally?

EG: You know, I came in having the one year under my belt and coming in with a bit more experience with age. I worked out hard this summer. Coming in stronger and faster has definitely been key.

HP: Now, you had the pleasure of playing in the Ivan Hlinka Tournament for Canada and were part of that gold medal winning team. And the year before you also won a gold medal. That's always a good feeling I would imagine.

EG: Absolutely. Those are definitely the experiences of a lifetime. I can't pinpoint one which is my favorite. Winning a gold medal for your country, wearing the red and the crest on your chest is definitely something special that not many kids get to do. So it was a great honor and I had a lot of fun with it.

HP: NHL Central Scouting came out with their initial rankings for OHL prospects. They have you at fourth among the OHL prospects–just a general thought on that.

EG: You know, I don't really think about it. I really make sure that I keep it in the back of my mind and leave it there. But it's nice to see I'm getting recognized. And I'm pretty high up there, but obviously that's not where I want to be. I want to be higher and I'm going to be working hard to achieve that.

HP: A lot of people, when they speak of you, talk about your leadership qualities, and I know you look up to your younger brother Dennis — who's been through the cancer battle a couple of times. When you see the type of leadership that he shows, to go through an experience like that, does it make it easy to be a leader on the ice?

EG: Absolutely. I mean, just taking into account what some kids have to go through in hospitals and stuff like that and just realizing how fortunate we are to be able to use all of our body completely, as it works. It's definitely something special and not many guys take that into account. But when it comes to on the ice– I want to just make sure that I'm not a follower and make sure that I'm showing the way for the guys is one of the biggest things.

HP: If you were giving a scouting report on yourself, how would you best describe your own game?

EG: I'd say that I'm pretty physical; I'm a good skater for my size. I just play with a lot of passion and a lot of heart–that's the biggest thing. I love the game and that's really important to how my game is played.

HP: Growing up, was there a player that you admired that was your favorite player and maybe even that you've emulated your game a little bit from?

EG: When I was younger, I always liked Scottie Niedermayer for his skating skills and defensive abilities and stuff like that. But to be honest with you, I've patterned my game around Dion Phaneuf; I believe that I'm a lot like him. He's very physical, he's a big man. He plays with a little edge and I'm trying to set myself up like that this year and play like him.

HP: Being from Orleans, Ontario, does that make you a Habs fan or does that make you an Ottawa Senators fan?

EG: Absolutely a Habs fan, absolutely a Habs fan. The first piece of clothing I ever wore was a Habs jersey out of the hospital.

HP: Coming in the season, did you set any particular goals personally for yourself or is it more of a help-the-team-win-at-all-costs type of thing?

EG: Well, I mean, absolutely—definitely the team first, that's always been my mentality but there's always been personal goals that I set for myself. I had set going to the World Juniors. Unfortunately, that didn't come. But in hockey not everything comes to you. I mean, I've set other goals and they're all very high.

HP: Now, you have the pleasure of having Doug Gilmour—a former NHL star—as the head coach of your club. This is his second season behind your bench. Have you seen a difference in how he's approaching things from year one to year two? And what he is like to have as a coach?

EG: Having him as a coach is definitely something special because he has all the experience in the world. He knows exactly what we're talking about when it comes to guys just being tired and stuff like that. But he's definitely come in more prepared this year. He's a lot more comfortable behind the bench. And he's coming with a game plan and that's definitely been important because last year—sometimes it was just mixing and matching. This year it's really: "we've got to follow this every game, game in and game out."

HP: Every player is always working on some aspect of their game to improve on. What's Erik Gudbranson working on to get a little bit better at?

EG: You know, I made sure this year that I was better defensively. I was pretty far in the minuses last year. This year I'm working myself up in the pluses, keeping myself defensively sound. Obviously now I'm taking a little bit more liberties offensively and I'm jumping up in the play a lot more so that's definitely been big.

HP: You're going to have the opportunity to play in the CHL Top Prospects game, given your ranking. Are we to assume that Gilmour has probably called Cherry to make sure you're on his club for the prospects game? Being from the Kingston Frontenacs and with Doug Gilmour as your coach, are you for sure on Team Cherry do you think?

EG: You know, I have no clue. I had the opportunity to meet Don a few times. He's a really nice guy and it would be an absolute honor to be there or be on Bobby's team. It's really not that big of a deal. The big thing is being at that game and playing well.

HP: I'm only teasing you. But yeah, Bobby Orr would be all right, too, being a defenseman. Obviously being in your draft, did you find any additional pressure over last year even?

EG: You know what? To be honest with you, going through my Minor Midget draft year was a lot tougher than this year, because I was new and I wasn't accustomed to scouts being in the stands and stuff like that. You know what? I know they're there and I really keep it in the back of my mind. As you said before, just playing for the Frontenacs is big. I'm not playing for the scouts; I'm playing for my hockey team.

HP: Give us a thought on what you think the Kingston Frontenacs might be capable of this year.

EG: A lot greater things than last year. I mean, we come in, we have a game plan, as I said and we're very skilled up front, we've got solid defense. And I mean, we're a lot tighter-knit group this year, so that's big.

Tyler Seguin

Center – Plymouth Whalers
Released on 17 November 2009

HP: Tyler, most scouting services and sources have you ranked either first or second for the upcoming NHL draft. That must be pretty gratifying as far as you've come in the last year.

TS: Definitely. My stock's been going up as the season has been going on. This season I really had a big goal of mine to come in with a strong start.

HP: Now you had a very good season last year, you had a point a game. But did you feel you had a little bit to prove? A lot of people it seems were whispering that you had two great line mates and that may have helped you, but you put that talk to rest a bit.

TS: Yeah. Well, definitely. All my friends kind of joke around with me just saying how they thought that was the reason why I started playing so well. I just wanted to prove people wrong and show that I don't need get line mates to do that and right now it's working.

HP: Now, you had the great experience at the Ivan Hlinka Tournament playing with Team Canada. What was the experience like for you?

TS: Well you know, anytime you get to represent your province or country, it's definitely a true honor and to share that experience and that gold medal with that group of guys is definitely a memory I'm going to treasure for the rest of my life.

HP: Now, you've worn the captaincy in a rotation with your team, the Plymouth Whalers this year. You're only 17 years old, but have you tried to take a more active role in leadership on that team?

TS: Well, you know it's always been my thing, try to be a leader the best I can on and off the ice. Right now at the beginning of the season, we've had some injuries. So we're kind of testing out different guys. That doesn't mean too much for me. I'm just going to go out there and be a leader no matter what.

HP: Have you been a little surprised at just how well you have done this year yourself or you had tremendous confidence in yourself?

TS: Well, I do have a lot of confidence in myself. I knew this summer coming in that I wanted to have a lot of points this year and have good team success and there was a goal in mind, just come out with a strong start. Right now I just want to keep consistency.

HP: Now, you've been compared to your idol, Steve Yzerman, as to how you play the game and certainly Steve took pride in the defensive side of his game toward the end of his career. Did you model your game after how he played?

TS: I think I did. I mean, growing up he was always my favorite player, just the way he played the game just being very good defensively, as well as offensively and also being a leader for the Detroit Red Wings. Last year I had an opportunity to meet him and that was a pretty cool thing. And yeah, I definitely play my game kind of like he did.

HP: Now, being from Brampton, Ontario, does that make a Toronto Maple Leafs fan growing up or were a Red Wing Fan with the Yzerman connection?

TS: Well, I think I didn't really have too much of a favorite team. Where I lived, Steve Yzerman was my favorite player but my favorite team was Toronto Maple Leafs and now that I'm here in Detroit, I get to go to all the Red Wings games and they have come to be my favorite team down here.

HP: Now the World Juniors, they're obviously up, coming after Christmas. Is that something that you have your sights firmly set on—getting an invite to the camp and perhaps making that club?

TS: Well, yeah for sure. Anytime when you're little as a kid you want to make the NHL and also represent your country at the World Juniors and all the stuff like that. I have the opportunity to go to the camp and the next month will be pretty cool, but I'm still waiting to hear.

HP: Now, obviously you're going to get to play in a lot of big games this year, including the CHL Top Prospects game. Are you excited to take part in that type of an event?

TS: Absolutely. Just again anytime you get to represent a province, country, or the OHL is something special and definitely going to take good pride in it.

HP: You have always had the great offensive instincts, but you really play a solid defensive game. Is that something that you work on in particular and take a lot of pride in?

TS: Yeah, especially at the end of last year and coming into this year. I talked to my coaches an realized that to get the next level you can't only just have skill and be able to put the puck in the net you also have to be a full, complete player and playing center—that's my role and that's what I want to do.

HP: Now, it's odd that your dad was almost a complete hockey opposite of yourself. He was a bit of a scrapper and you have more of a finesse game.

TS: That's kind of funny. I mean, when I was young my dad started me off as a defenseman, but then after sometime realized that I was good at going and making plays and realized I should be a forward. You know, my dad also has speed so I think that's something that we both have in common. But other than that, he was kind of, like you said the opposite of me.

HP: Every player is always working on a different aspect of their game, trying to improve. Is there something in particular that you have been focusing on, trying to get a little better, heading toward the draft?

TS: Last year I had always been playmaker and this year I think I'm trying to show scouts that I can also bury the puck. Right now I'm not really used to it but I kind of had more goals than I do assists. But mainly right now my main focus is improving my defensive zone.

HP: Do you find that all the talk between yourself and Cam Fowler and Taylor Hall, is that kind of enjoyable to hear the banter back and forth about who's going to go No. 1?

TS: Oh, yeah. It's pretty good. It's a good accomplishment, but I also know that it's very early in the season and I can't let all the media and people talking get to my head. I just really got to be in the back of my head and just focus on what my game is and let the scouts decide all that stuff.

HP: Your coach, Mike Vellucci, is one of the veteran coaches in his league. Obviously when he took back over at the bench last season, he really turned your game around, giving you a lot more playing time. What's he like to play under?

TS: I mean he's a great coach. He always gives me constructive criticism. I mean, if I go down and make a goal but I make a bad defensive play to start the play off, he'll let me know that and I really appreciate that kind of stuff.

HP: What do you look at with Plymouth? They're obviously in a dog fight in the Western Conference with a couple of team that are juggernauts at the moment anyway, but lots of skill it looks like on that club.

TS: Yeah, definitely. We have a lot of heart and passion. And there's good teams in the Western Conference. So I think some teams might underestimate us. So I think maybe we can be the black horse of the division.

Tyler Toffoli
RW/C – Ottawa 67's
Released on 09 November 2009

HP: Tyler, you started a little bit slow this year but your offence is starting to crank up a little bit in the last few games.

TT: Yeah, I know. The bounces have not been going my way so far. I know early in the season I was kind of gripping the stick a little tight but now the puck's going in the net for me and I'm playing a lot better than I was at the start of the year.

HP: Now obviously you're draft eligible— probably one of the highest-ranked prospects in the Ontario Hockey League, although nothing's come out for rankings yet. Do you feel any pressure about that at all?

TT: No. You know, you just kind of go there and play your own game and not worry about that stuff. I mean, the draft isn't until the end of the year. So there's a lot of time, so you can't really think about it and just play your game.

HP: Now you have a history of putting up a lot of offense back with the Toronto Junior Canadiens coming into this league: you had 174 points with John McFarland, who went first in the OHL Draft, while you went seventh. Last year you had a good season. Did you put any expectations on yourself as to what you'd like to accomplish this year?

TT: No. I just want to have a great season. In the end, I just want my team to do well—that's what comes first and then the points will come and all the rest of the stuff will come. But I just want my team to do well and to go far in the playoffs and that's all that matters.

HP: Now in the summer you had a neat experience getting to play in the Ivan Hlinka Tournament for Canada. What was that experience like for you?

TT: It was a lot of fun. The whole team gelled together as one; we're just a big family. I mean, we're there for almost a month and that's all we had is just the other guys on the team. So we kind of came together and we ended up winning the tournament. It was a lot of fun.

HP: Now you recently got named to the 2009 Super Series team for the Ontario Hockey League. What does that mean to you?

TT: Oh, it was a surprise. I mean, I didn't really think too much about it. I didn't even know too much about it at all. And then my agent and my parents told me and I was just really excited and just to get the chance to play against the Russians again. I mean, I got the chance at the Under-18 in the final game. So hopefully I can bring my winning ways to that.

HP: Growing up, is there somebody in particular—an NHL player—that you've patterned yourself game-wise after?

TT: No, I haven't really done any of that. But I've heard things about being compared to Heatley and Cheechoo and stuff like that. So I just try to play my game and just go from there.

HP: Your assistant coach from last year, Chris Byrne, has taken over from a legend in his own right—Hall of Famer, Brian Kilrea. What's the transition been like for you?

TT: Oh, it hasn't been too tough. I mean, the coaching style is a lot different. I mean, Kilrea just kind of told you how it was and Byrne just makes you work and just work and work and work and that's that. It's good. I mean, the team's all fitting in now. I mean, we've been playing a lot better since he started here so it's been good.

HP: Every player is obviously working on an aspect of their game, trying to refine it a little bit more. Is there something in particular in your game that you're working a little bit harder on?

TT: You know, I'm just working on my skating. I mean, people say that my skating's not bad but it needs work. My quick stride is to get myself going and that's about all I'm working on.

HP: When you look back at the history of the Ottawa 67's—in the recent history—they produced a lot of players that have gone onto the National Hockey League or on the cusp of it: your own teammate, Tyler Cuma, first round pick; of course, Logan Couture; and Jamie McGinn in the not so distant past. Does that give you a lot of hope that this is quite a development situation for you?

TT: Yeah. I mean, I know they're all hard workers. I know Cuma works hard every single day, day in and day out. So I kind just try and work my way like that and hopefully I get drafted in the first round all the good stuff comes along with it.

HP: It always seems like every year it's kind of exciting to play in the CHL Top Prospects Game. You're obviously—barring you get hurt or something—going to get that chance. Is that exciting to you—that you get to play in front of that type of situation?

TT: Yeah, I'm really excited. I mean, right now I've got to finish the rest of the season before that and everything else—the Super Series and all that stuff. So I'm thinking about it, just playing my game and will try and get myself into that game.

HP: The 67's have started a little bit slow this year. But can you give us a read on what type of team you see this as?

TT: Oh, I think we're a great team. I mean, we have a lot of skill. Our defense is really good and the offense is coming. I mean we're just buying into our systems as Byrne is putting at us, too. So hopefully all that comes quick and soon so we can get a good season going and just go from there.

Geoffrey Schemitsch
Defense – Owen Sound Attack
Released on 30 January 2010

HP: Speaking with Owen Sound Attack defenseman, Geoffrey Schemitsch. Geoff, you're a bit of a surprise in the Ontario Hockey League this year. Nobody knew too much about you, you came in and you had been committed to the Vaughan Vipers and came into training camp and earned yourself a spot. It's been a storybook year for you so far.

GS: Yeah, so far. I mean, I was just looking to probably play Tier II this year and came to Owen Sound and found a good opportunity to play and things have just worked out so far.

HP: Is it true you more or less came to camp just for the experience, hoping that would help you with your old club and suddenly you're here in the OHL?

GS: Yeah. I think I was basically going for the experience; I wasn't really expecting anything. But I came there, I played well, and I thought this could really be a good opportunity for me and I took it.

HP: You've been among the rookie leaders in scoring, certainly among defensemen and actually all scorers in the Ontario Hockey League for most of the season. What's been the key to accomplishing what you've done so far?

GS: Well, I just try to play my game and hopefully things will come to me, I try to contribute a bit offensively, work the power play, and things just fall into place I think.

HP: You're ranked 169th by NHL Central Scouting. Hockeyprospect.com has you listed at number 52 on their list, which will put you in the second round. But for a guy that didn't expect to play in the Ontario Hockey League, you have to be happy you're on any list?

GS: Yeah, for sure. I mean, especially I wasn't expecting to be on any sort of list this year and I guess guys have just taken notice of me playing well and it's good to get some recognition.

HP: Do you have an NHL player that you pattern your game after at all?

GS: I wouldn't say that I try and pattern my game after, but a guy I look up to is a guy probably like Duncan Keith from Chicago. He plays a really good two-way game and contributes at both ends of the ice so he's the guy I look to, I guess.

HP: People do say you play very well in all three zones, scouts say that. In terms of working on your game, what are you working on in particular to refine with your game as we head down the stretch here?

GS: I'm trying to get stronger. I mean, you just got to be strong, working with a lot of the bigger guys in the league along the boards and in the corner, so I just feel like I need to. I'm trying to work on that throughout the season and just try and get better at that.

HP: Now, you have the pleasure of having a couple players on this team as well. They're also ranked for the NHL draft and going through the same sort of process as you. Does that make it a little easier to take the pressure off yourself with a couple other guys—Hishon and Shipley going through the same thing?

GS: Yeah, for sure. I mean, Hish & Ship have been great to me. They're unbelievable players themselves and you know, it's just great having them around, guys you can talk to and things like that. And also the guys who have been through it before, like Jesse Blacker and you know it's really a big help having guys around like that trying and just to talk to you when things aren't going your way and take a little bit of pressure off you as well.

HP: Now, you're from Thornhill, Ontario, which is in the GTA. Does that naturally make you at Toronto Maple Leaf fan at all or no?

GS: Yeah, I'd say so. I've been a big Leaf fan all my life, so I guess so.

HP: Well, nothing wrong with that. I think most people around here are. But I'm sure you will be happy to be drafted by any of the other 29 teams as well.

GS: Oh, yeah, for sure. That would just be probably one of the greatest moments of my life, if I could get drafted by any club.

HP: Now, you play against some of the high-end players that are ranked first and second: Taylor Hall and Tyler Seguin. Being a defenseman, you have to play against those guys regularly. What can you say about each of those guys that makes them at the top level of the draft?

GS: Well, actually I wasn't in the last game against Plymouth, but I mean Seguin looks like he's going to be a great player. I mean, he's got great speed, he sees the ice well, and always makes good plays in the offensive zone. And then, playing against Hall, I mean he's probably one of the fastest players I've ever played against. His creativity is unbelievable—the things that he can do with the puck. So they're going to be great players themselves and it's tough to play against them.

HP: The Owen Sound Attack team has gotten healthy all of a sudden and you're back in the lineup, I understand, tonight as well after being out a little bit. But how good is this Attack team do you think?

GS: I think that we can compete with any club in the league. When we stick to our systems, we got everyone in. If we just do what coach wants us to do, things will just happen for us.

HP: You've come a long way this year. Do you have any advice for young guys that are trying to get to the same level as yourself?

GS: Just keep working hard and always try to improve your game is basically the main thing that you've got to do. If you don't get drafted, just keep looking to make it and hopefully someone will see you.

Trevor Parkes

RW – Montreal Juniors
Released on November 12, 2009

HP: Speaking with right winger Trevor Parkes of the Montreal Juniors and Trevor happens to be the CHL Player of the Week this week for his performance. First of all, Trevor, you must be quite thrilled with getting that honor.

TP: Yeah, definitely. It's a big honor to get. I'm really proud of myself. Just having a good week, just trying to win every single battle and the points came and it was a good week for me.

HP: Now, you're off to a real strong start, coming in from Fort Erie Meteors Junior League last year. You've got 13 goals and 20 points in 22 games. You went undrafted in the Ontario Hockey League draft twice. Then you had to clear waivers to go to the Quebec League—they didn't take you there, either. How have you been able to do what you've done so far?

TP: I've just always been kind of put down and been doubted by a lot of people, so now when I get my chance to prove people wrong, it feels good to show them. I'm just working hard and I'm glad I am where I am right now and just want to keep it up.

HP: What's been going right with your game so far this season?

TP: It's going great. I'm getting that period of getting played a lot right now, I've just been working hard and the goals have come...I got a little bit of a slump there, about ten game mark and I just try to go back to the basics a bit. And now it's starting to come off for me.

HP: Now, you had 23 goals and 43 points last year in 52 games for Fort Erie. But interestingly enough, only nine points on the power play so you didn't get much of a chance to play the special teams. Did you have this belief that you could step in at this level and perform like you are?

TP: Yeah, definitely. Last year I started out playing the power play a bit in the Fort Erie games in the conference. Right away when I came here, they gave me a chance start on the power play and that gave me confidence in myself. Now I definitely feel like I can play the power play in this league and I'm happy to do it.

HP: Now, how have you found the adjustment to playing in Montreal versus being in Ontario, just with the language and the culture? Has it been interesting for you?

TP: Yeah, it's definitely a lot different than being back home in Fort Erie, just different language going on—you got half the team speaking French, half the team speaking English. But sometimes when you're on the ice, you just got to forget about all that's around you and just focus on playing hockey.

HP: Now, as an untypical older first year player, such that you are, do you feel that you've taken on a bit of a leadership role in that club at all?

TP: Oh, yeah definitely. There's a lot of younger rookies right now. I'm also in the same class with them but I'm trying to help some of the younger guys also, even though I am a rookie. You just got to show maturity. Some of the other guys are kind of helping them out. I'm also been getting helped out from the older guys I'm watching, so it's all working out.

HP: Now, who do you compare your style of game to in the NHL? A player your style kind of reminds of?

TP: I've been told a Jordan Staal kind of guy. I like to play a bit more offensively than Jordan Staal, more like he's a third line shutdown role, but he's a big player. I use my body to help me out but I just try to put the puck in there as much as I can too, so I'm kind of like him.

HP: Now, being from Fort Erie, Ontario, were you typically like a Leaf fan growing up, or did you cheer for a different team?

TP: Yeah, I've always been a typical Leaf fan growing up. When you say that, you get all the boo's. But being up here surprised me. I've turned into a Canadiens fan. I like what they've got going on with Gomez, Gionta, and Cammalleri But yeah, I'm typically a Leaf fan from back home.

HP: Have you used the motivation of rejection from the whole OHL and probably people have been telling you that you can't do this for a long time. Has that been a real motivator for you?

TP: Yeah, it's actually a huge motivator for me. Every day I just step on the ice just thinking that people doubted me my whole life growing up through hockey and I never really got an opportunity. Now that I've got that opportunity, I'm going to take it and run with it because it just proves people wrong and I'm really happy I got the opportunity.

HP: Now, nobody really knows a whole lot about you obviously. You've kind of come in a whirlwind. What can you tell us about yourself? I mean, what do you like to do off the ice?

TP: Off the ice I enjoy working out, keeping in shape. I also enjoy a lot of other sports. Like back home I'm always active and playing school sports like school volleyball, Lacrosse, soccer, so anything to do with sports. I like watching NHL games, so most things involved in sports. I always like to stay active.

HP: Now, you currently lead all Quebec league rookies in goals and you have a 24.5 shooting percentage. What do you attribute that to?

TP: I just shoot the puck. I've been told back home by coaches, you know Broussard always said I got good shot and I got to use it. So, taking my time and placing the shoot, not just shooting anything. Do anything for a higher chance, you got to put the puck toward the net. Like when Wayne Gretzky always said: "100% of the shots you don't take, don't go in the net." So I just put the puck towards the net and anything can happen to you.

HP: I talked to an NHL scout who told me you really have a knack of getting your shot off in stride. Is that one of the reasons you think you're getting so many goals?

TP: Yeah, it's definitely a big thing. Growing up I always heard that, I was always told to work on that—getting your shot off in stride. One thing is the goalie is not going to expect it. When you stop moving your feet, the goalie has time to prepare and get ready for the shot. So if you can get that shot off in stride, you're always going to catch the goalie off guard and you got a great chance to put the puck in the net.

HP: Now, you're team is in a tough division. You're sitting in third spot in your division, a game over .500. How do you size up your club?

TP: We're a really young club and I think we're coming along. We had a pretty good start going on there. We've kind of slumped a bit, but this weekend we also two games in our own division. If we can win both those games, we move up to second spot. And we also beat Gatineau last weekend, the top team in our division. So I think at the end of the year we can be at the top of our division. We got a young club and I think as we build toward the season we should have a good team.

Brandon Gormley
Defense – Moncton Wildcats
Released on 03 March 2010

HP: How is your season going so far?

BG: It's going pretty good. We've got a good team here and everyone is playing great and really coming together after some pickups.

HP: As a top prospect, how have you balanced approaching the draft and just playing through the season?

BG: You really can't pay to much attention to it. Everyone is going to have their opinion of you and how you play so you got to go out and play your game and not think about what the scouts and rankings are saying.

HP: When you are on the ice, how do you like to contribute?

BG: I think I contribute in a lot of ways. I take pride in playing in all situations and being the go to guy out there, you want to be on the power play, penalty kill and five on five as well.

HP: How was your experience at the CHL top prospects game?

BG: The Top Prospects game was great. It's a good experience and always fun to see your buddies again. It's important though as its one game that can show everyone what you got so you want to be at your best.

HP: Who are some of the stronger forwards you've played against?

BG: There's been a lot of them. I played against Taylor Hall at the Top Prospects game. It's tough, lots of good players in our league, and playing at world junior camp was a challenge as well.

HP: What was your goal going into the season?

BG: I just wanted to help the team win. You need to do whatever you can to help the team win. We've got a great team here and we are looking to make a good playoff run here. I had to put the draft and all that in the back of my mind and focus on winning.

HP: What do you think will be most important for you to improve on in order to make the NHL?

BG: I think strength and conditioning. That's one of the big things in today's game. You can have all the skill in the world, but if you're not ready to play against big guys, you aren't going to have success.

HP: Are there any players you look up to?

BG: I look up to Nick Lidstrom. I try to model my game after him. He has been one of the best players in the league for many years. Just have to be smart and use my skills.

HP: Can you talk about your transition into the Q and various challenges?

BC: I think I made a pretty smooth entry. Like I said, it's a really good league. I got a chance to play with Mark Barberio and he is one of the best defenseman in our league. Coming into the league at 16, not a lot of guys get to play with a guy at the caliber like that, so he made my transition easier. Last year, like I said, I was playing against older, bigger, stronger players and your size at 16 is not up to the par with 19/20 year olds so that was a challenge.

HP: So, right now, is the main focus winning the Memorial Cup?

BC: For sure, it's the ultimate goal. We are one of the top junior teams in league, and got a good group of guys to make a room.

Louis Marc Aubry

Center – Montreal Juniors
Released on 11 February 2010

HP: How's your season going so far?

LMA: The second (half) of the season is going good, the last couple games. Overall I've had a pretty good season.

HP: What do you think you've improved on last season?

LMA: I've gained weight since last season so I'm stronger and finish my checks.

HP: Many consider you a smart, big centerman and a three-zone player. How do you think your skill set and size does it make you more attractive to scouts?

LMA: Yeah, I want to be a strong two-way center and play well in both ends in the ice. Good defensively and do some things offensively as well.

HP: What do you think you can attribute your increased point totals to?

LMA: Last season was my first season, and we were a good team so I wasn't playing too much. This season I knew I wanted to get more points with more time and I've already done better than last year. I try not to think about points and more about overall performance. I think scouts check how you play more than stats.

HP: In terms of playing strong, where do you play your best?

LMA: I'm good in my own zone, I can get the puck out. I can find my teammates in the offensive zone.

HP: More of a playmaker then a shooter?

LMA: Yeah, but I like to get in front of the net to score. Tip pucks and get rebounds in front of the net to score.

HP: On draft day, why will they be drafting you?

LMA: A big centerman who can play on both ends of the ice. I can be strong defensively and bring something offensively as well.

HP: Any players in the NHL currently you look up to?

LMA: Yeah , Jordan Staal. I like to compare myself to him.

HP: What do you want to improve on most throughout the season?
LMA: I just want to have a strong finish. Last year, I had a strong finish as well, and it helps me improve. I want to improve and work hard every day and just have a strong end of the season and big series.

HP: What has been the highlight of your career so far?

LMA: Last year, because of injuries in the playoffs, we won the first round in the playoffs and I got to play a lot. A lot of the older talented guys got hurt, and the younger guys like me had to step up.

HP: If you attend a training camp, what would you try and accomplish there?

LMA: I'll just play my game. I'll do the same thing that they drafted me for.

Jeff Skinner
Center – Kitchener Rangers
Released on 03 February 2010

HP: How's your season going?

JS: It's going good so far. We are hitting the stretch here where points are at a premium so it should be fun heading into the playoffs

HP: What's been different this year than your first year in the OHL?

JS: I'm just more comfortable in all situations. Being my second year, I know more about what the league has to offer and what situations you can be put into. I think I'm more of a leader and just more comfortable.

HP: In terms of being a leader, is that something that you think elevates your game?

JS: Yeah I think so. I think that extra responsibility is something I pride myself on. You always want to do whatever you can to help the team win, so if I'm looked to as a leader, that is how I have to play.

HP: When most people look at your game, they are going to think goal scoring. What do you think accounts for most of your production in that area?

JS: Firstly I have to give a lot of credit to my teammates for finding me. But, I like to think most of my goals are hard working goals and a result of competing.

HP: Do you think you have a knack for finding the right spots on the ice to score?

JS: Yeah I like to think that. I think having that ability to skate into the right spots is sometimes lucky and sometimes getting to where you think the puck is going to be and other times it's your teammates finding you. So, I think it's a combination of all those things.

HP: What do you think has been the biggest improvement in your game since last season?

JS: Well, my offensive production is higher this year, but overall I think I've improved my whole game. I'm bigger and faster, and when you come into the league you realize these players are a lot smarter. I think knowing what to expect has improved my game.

HP: Would you say you've become a smarter player or think the game better?

JS: Yeah definitely

HP: Why do you think a GM is going to draft you in June

JS: I hope it's because he wants someone who competes hard and work hard every shift each and every day. I like to be a guy who can be counted on to produce offensively, so hopefully those things.

HP: What's your goal for the rest of the season beyond putting up numbers.

JS: It is to go for a long playoff run and see how far we can get. I think we have a really talented team so I think we can do some good things in the playoffs.

Quinton Howden

LW – Moose Jaw Warriors
Released on 29 January 2010

HP: Just to start things off, Do you have any thoughts on your play last season?

QH: Last season was good, we had a rough time as a team, but we got the season done, and coming back this year it was important that we got off to a good start; we've been doing good so far, so we're on the right track.

HP: How would you say you've improved from last season?

QH: I think my hard work. I'm putting in the effort to get the breaks I'm getting. I do a lot of things behind the scenes to improve my game on the ice; I take everything into factor and try to do the best I can.

HP: What sort of things do you learn from your mistakes?

QH: Everything. That's the only way that you can learn in life; learning from your mistakes. Things I do on the ice or off the ice; I try to think about them and turn everything into positives. You turn them into negatives, that's when you start playing bad and you're not yourself. If I can turn everything into positives and keep on the right track everything should be alright.

HP: You've had a great season so far, you might double the number of points you got last season, who or what would you credit for your success?

QH: I'm getting a chance to play with some great guys like [Jason Bast] and [Thomas Frazee], they're phenomenal line mates and I can learn so much from both of them; they've been through more than anybody. I try to take things from them and help them out as much as I can, and they're doing the same for me. The main part is we're having fun out there, and it's enjoyable and at the same time we're working hard.

HP: Last season, your plus minus was at a disappointing minus thirty seven, but this season thus far you're a plus fifteen, what's changed from last season to this season?

QH: I've worked a lot on my defensive zone. That's one of the things I try to work a lot on; my play away from the puck. In the defensive zone I've done a lot better with having my stick on the ice, and being aware of where guys are at.

Just the little things I can do to try and improve myself, it's helped my plus minus from last year. I've just been taking stuff from the leaders and trying to take everything into factor and build up on everything.

HP: What do you hope to achieve from now until the end of the season? Do you have any short term goals?

QH: Yeah, I want to go as far as I can with our team, that's my main goal. I set little goals for myself along the way, but those can't be accomplished without team accomplishment, so the farther we can go as a team, that's all I want. I'll do all I can for that to help everybody out and help them get as far as they can.

HP: You're a big player at 6' 3'', and you're also a great skater; how do you use your body and speed to your advantage on the ice?

QH: I have a big body and if I can throw it around when I need to, be physical, and get guys off the puck. My speed is definitely one of my biggest assets, whenever I get a chance to get a burst of speed an get going; it's something I look for each time I'm on the ice. When I can do that, I can create space for myself and look for my open line mates and maybe accomplish something.

HP: What NHL player if any would you compare your game to?

QH: I think I'd compare myself kind of like a Patrick Marleau type guy, he's a great leader on and off the ice, he's a big physical guy, and he works hard every day and night, night in and night out, if I can pattern myself after him, it'd be a great honour, and I'd love to mold myself up to his play.

HP: Have you tried to take on a leadership role on your team?

QH: Yeah, I try to do as much as I can to bring guys up and being on the right level. It's a team game, so the farthest we can go as a team, and the most I can help out at, results in doing our best.

HP: You seem to know what you're doing out there, but what parts of your game are you looking to improve on?

QH: I think just sticking to the page, we've had some rough games the last while, all the other teams have kind of outplayed us, but I think that if we stick to the page and we all do what we're capable of doing, we should be fine.

HP: What sort of things do you do off the ice? Do you have any hobbies?

QH: Yeah, I've been working out everyday, I'm trying to get myself ready for on ice and the future, but off the ice I just like to hang out with some of the guys, relax when I can, get out and do some golfing and stuff when I can. I love to golf and I'm always doing activities and stuff and getting involved with as many people as I can.

HP: If you were running an NHL team, why would you draft a player like yourself?

QH: Because I think I'm a valuable guy to have on a team. I work hard, and can bring some leadership to a team. I have some big assets that any team can use as far as my speed and vision and stuff like that, so I if I can bring that to a team, that'd be huge for me.

Dylan McIlrath

Defense – Moose Jaw Warriors
Released on 27 Jan 2010

HP: How was the experience at the Top Prospects game and Why do you think your draft stock has increased so much?

DM: It was a great experience playing with all that high level of talent and getting to know them on a personal level. It was cool meeting Bobby Orr and Don Cherry. The whole thing was kind of surreal, it was one of the first things I've ever been to with all that media. I think my stock has risen because I bring a physical element and can stick up for my team mates when needed. I guess that's what the scouts are looking for and it has helped me this year. I think I improved a lot this summer with my foot speed and getting bigger and stronger.

HP: Do you think recent early success of tough, young players such as Milan Lucic or James Neal has helped your stock?

DM: Yeah, I try to stick with my role. I'm not going to be a top scorer and I know that, so I'm trying to play my role. I keep it simple, chip pucks, get it in deep, not do anything too crazy, be physical and I think I can do that at the next level to.

HP: Did Don Cherry or Bobby Orr have any pieces of advice for you at the Top Prospects game because of your unique skill set for the tourney?

DM: I was talking to Bobby Orr and he really liked my game after I fought, he thought that was cool. I just tried to take whatever I could after them. They are really well known around the NHL and hockey world, so I tried to pick their brains. Any chance I got to talk to Bobby Orr, I took as a great honor.

HP: What has accounted for your improved +/- this year?

DM: I think as a team we struggled a lot last season and that had to do with it. This year, I worked a lot on my defensive game. My goal is not to get scored on so when I get out against the top players I try and shut them down. I worked on my offensive game so I can get more pluses than minuses.

HP: Now that you've shot up the draft rankings so much, what is your goal for the rest of the season?

DM: Keep getting better and make myself more of a complete player to catch the scouts eyes by continuing to play my game.

HP: Any players you look up to?

DM: Some players I looked up to are Shea Weber and Dion Phaneuf, Chris Pronger. Shut down D-men that bring the physical element.

HP: If you are at an NHL training camp next year, what about your game will catch the management's eye?

DM: I have to be physical even at a pro camp. I can't be soft, because they are bigger, stronger and more experienced. I have to do what I do best, play to my role and hope they notice that.

HP: Being a physical, aggressive player, with the onslaught of recent hits to the head, how do you keep your game in control so you are not risking the safety of other players?

DM: Yeah I just don't try and run around and kill guys. I hit them at the right time, when they are coming down the wall, I finish my checks. I don't try to hit dirty, I just be a physical factor. In terms of hits to head, I make sure I'm not getting my elbows up. Even though I'm a bigger guy hitting smaller guys, I keep my shoulders down. It's the game of hockey, accidents will happen, but I limit it by keeping my shoulders down and knowing my surroundings.

HP: Any NHL players you aspire to fight?
DM: Haven't thought about it yet, but we'll see.

Emerson Etem

Medicine Hat Tigers
Released on 26 January 2010

HP: So, you grew up in Long Beach California. Was hockey popular there? What inspired you to start playing hockey?

EE: My brother played hockey when I was younger; I was about three at the time. There was just a little roller rink down the street and he was playing so I just joined in not too long after. Then when I got bigger, I just switched to ice and ever since then I just played youth hockey in California.

HP: I read something about you playing roller hockey before ice, you began playing ice hockey when you were six?

EE: Yeah

HP: You've grown and gotten a lot better. What was going through your head when you were drafted in 07 in the Bantam Draft?

EE: It was the biggest thing for me; it wasn't about the round or whatever organization I went to. Medicine Hat; I knew it was great, I knew the coaching was great, and the fans here are the best in the league, so that was the most important thing for me.

HP: How did you feel about the U.S. Under 18 National team?

EE: It was a good experience, I had great coaches there. It was obviously a short time there, but I learned a lot and got physically bigger and more mature for [the WHL]. It was a good year for me to just work on my skills and like I said; prepare for this year.

HP: You've had a really good season so far. You're averaging more than a point per game; what or who would you credit for having such a successful first season in the Western Hockey League

EE: I can't really think of one person; I think I have a lot of people to thank and so many people that have helped me out get to this point. I think the U.S. program helped me out a lot, their coaching staff and their hockey program helped me out a lot, and now I'm here and having a great time, and the coaching staff has been really good to me here, so I think I'm playing pretty well to go along with it.

HP: Coming from the U.S National Development program, how have you been able to adjust to WHL hockey?

EE: I took that year to get physically stronger, and I think that was the most important thing for me. I just think my overall skill development from the program has just made me a better player. I think pre-season helped a lot; early I needed to know how to succeed at this level, and just have that mindset of being consistent at every game, and playing at my top performance every game, it's just important for me, obviously you can't run that every game, but you try after that and I think I've been doing pretty well thus far.

HP: You have a big body and you use it a lot doing a great job protecting the puck, are there other things you're looking to use your big body for?

EE: Yeah, just driving hard to the net, being around the net, using my body to screen the goalie, I just like being around the net and use my body presence there. I still need to work on getting shots through from the shooting lanes and that kind of stuff, but I think that's what I'm good at and I just need to start finishing my checks better and that's what I want to use my body for, for the most part.

HP: How do you deal with other big guys pushing you around, you're a pretty big guy yourself, but there are other guys that try to push you around and get under your skin, how do you deal with guys like that?

EE: I just try to use my body to protect the puck as much as possible. There are big guys on every team and in this league it's full of big guys and that's why I always try to work on my strength, conditioning, and that kind of stuff, but for the most part I just try to use my body to shield the puck and try to get in scoring areas with my body.

HP: Are there any parts of your game you'd like to improve on?

EE: Yeah, finishing checks, playing a physical game is definitely the biggest thing I need to work on. Also getting shots through the shooting lanes and blocking shots and that kind of stuff, and I'm still working on it.

HP: The NHL Entry Draft is coming up in a few months, what do you think you bring to an NHL team?

EE: I think my speed. A lot of people are looking at that, and I think there's so much stuff that comes around my speed. I like to look for options on the rush or make options for my team-mates, I like to be around the net and use my skills to put the puck in the back of the net. I think I'd do that in many ways and like I said; use my speed.

Hopefully teams like that and whatever team that thinks I have the most value is the team I want to go to.

HP: Are there any long or short term goals you hope to achieve?

EE: Well, I obviously came to this league to try and make the NHL as soon as possible. I think there are a lot of things I still have to work on, but I think that's of them, being [in the NHL] as soon as possible and I'll do whatever it takes, and I'll work on my game to achieve that goal.

HP: Where do you see yourself five years from now?

EE: I definitely see myself in the NHL. Like I said, I need to work on a lot of things, but I want to play, I want to be a player in the NHL and make that my profession and within the next five years for sure. So I'm going to do whatever it takes to get there.

HP: What are your goals for the rest of the season?

CC: I just want to lead my team to a good playoff position and win a round or two in the playoffs. I want to get other guys noticed by some schools to and develop the program.

Mark Pysyk
Defense – Edmonton Oil Kings
Released on 21 December 2009

HP: Besides the obvious stats increase this season, what else has gone well for you so far in Edmonton?

MP: I think just playing with more confidence, playing with more ice time. When you are out there more, you can play every shift and not worry about making mistakes as much, you can go out there and play your own game. The coaches have confidence in you and you can have confidence in yourself to make the right plays.

HP: When you entered the Junior A ranks, what did you have to work on the most?

MP: I think foot speed, size and strength. That will come with time I guess, got to work out in the gym every summer. I also need to work on moving the puck quick, getting my shots off faster and harder.

HP: What are you most confident about in your game?

MP: I think my ability to read the ice and knowing where guys are all the time. I think I'm a good skater too, but can always improve.

HP: What has been more nerve wracking, waiting to get drafted to the WHL or the NHL?

MP: I think this one (NHL) is more nervous but you have more games. It is close, but this is the NHL. There is pressure, but it is only what you put on yourself. You can't just forget about it, but the more you can keep that out your game the better.

HP: What do you hope to accomplish once the season is over?

MP: Hopefully get drafted, have a good spring camp with them and maybe get a contract with them in a year or two.

HP: Who do you most compare your game to or model your game after?

MP: That's tough, but maybe Shea Weber. I model myself after a guy like that, I try to model my game after that. He is offensive, but plays well in his own zone.

HP: You have Shea Weber's shot yet?

MP: Not yet, but I'm working on it.

HP: It looks like you are going to be playing in the CHL Top Prospects game, are you excited for that?

MP: Yeah, I talked to my agent the other day about that. For now I'm just focusing on the games for us (Edmonton), but if that comes out of it, it'll be a great opportunity.

HP: Fast forward to draft day. A lot of people have you slated between 10-20, is it something that would bother you if you slip a little.

MP: It's just to get drafted and go from there. It's about getting to a training camp. You can't put too much pressure on yourself. It's a good thing to go higher, but either way you've got to work.

HP: What do you think about your game has most impressed NHL scouts.?

MP: The way I see the ice and my ability to make the right play.

For more player interviews including Taylor Hall and Cam Fowler visit HockeyProspect.com

3

NHL TEAM REPORTS

If a player has played or is expected to play one full season in the NHL (such as John Tavares or Evander Kane) they will not be included in the Top Five

ANAHEIM DUCKS:

The Anaheim Ducks have some strong defensive prospects, but lack a sure thing in their forward corps. 2009 draftee Peter Holland has a nice skill set and size, but is still a project player. He did have his good moments this season, but was mired by inconsistency. The defense is highlighted by two, first line potential players, in Luca Sbisa (in the WHL and played for the Swiss WJC team along with the Olympic team) and Jake Gardiner (a member of the USA WJC championship team and a key component to a dominant University of Wisconsin-Madison defensive corps). They lack depth at wing and center.

Possible First Round Targets:
1. Ryan Johansen
2. Austin Watson
3. Nick Bjugstad

Anaheim's Top-Five:
1. Luca Sbisa (Defense, Lethbridge/Portland WHL)
2. Jake Gardiner (Defense, Wisconsin NCAA)
3. Peter Holland (Forward, Guelph OHL)
4. Brandon McMillan (Forward, Kelowna WHL)
5. Nick Palmieri (Forward, Notre Dame NCAA

ATLANTA THRASHERS:

After trading Ilya Kovalchuk, the Thrashers will begin relying more and more on their prospect depth as they try to re-build. The good thing is they now look to have two picks in the first round. Unfortunately, one can argue that Atlanta's previous picks have not resulted in strong organizational depth. With their two first round picks, the Thrashers should simply go for the best two players available.

Possible First Round Targets:
1. Nino Niederreiter
2. Ryan Johansen
3. Brandon Gormley

Atlanta's Top Five:
1. Jeremy Morin (Forward, Kitchener OHL)
2. Carl Klingberg (Forward, Vastra Frolunda SEL)
3. Ivan Vishnevskiy (Defense, Chicago AHL)
4. Patrice Cormier (Forward, N/A QMJHL)
5. Artus Kulda (Defense, Chicago AHL)

BOSTON BRUINS:

The Bruins recently graduated elite goaltender Tuukka Rask and scrappy center Vladimir Sobotka to Boston. However they are still quite deep, especially at the center position in their prospect ranks. The Bruins prospect pool looks to get even deeper as they possess Toronto's top pick in this year's draft, along with their own first pick.

The Bruins need defensive depth but, with Toronto's pick should look to simply the best player available. Their 2nd overall pick will be who-ever is left between Hall and Seguin after Edmonton selects.

Possible First Round Targets
1. Taylor Hall
2. Tyler Seguin

1. Jarred Tinordi
2. Steven Johns

Boston's Top Five:
1. Joe Colborne (Forward, Denver NCAA)
2. Jordan Caron (Forward, Rimouski/Rouyn-Noranda QMJHL)
3. Brad Marchand (Forward, Providence AHL)
4. Yuri Alexandrov (Defense, Cherepovets KHL)
5. Zach Hamill (Forward, Providence AHL)

BUFFALO SABRES:

The Sabres must be thrilled with their scouting department considering the impact rookie Tyler Myers has had on the backend since they drafted him 13th overall in 2008. He should be a #1 defenseman for Buffalo for many years to come. In 2009 the Sabres added bruising power forward Zack Kassian to the mix at 13th overall, as well.

However, beyond Kassian, the Sabres forward prospects are quite small, highlighted by Tyler Ennis, Tim Kennedy and Nathan Gerbe: all skilled players, but it remains to be seen if they can become first line NHL players. Both Gerbe and Ennis have been highly productive in the AHL, while Kennedy is learning the ropes at the NHL level.

Possible First Round Target
1. Tyler Toffoli
2. Dylan McIlrath
3. Brock Nelson

Buffalo's Top Five:
1. Tyler Ennis (Forward, Portland AHL)
2. Jhonas Enroth (Goaltender, Portland AHL)
3. Luke Adam (Forward, Cape Breton QMJHL)
4. Zach Kassian (Forward, Windsor OHL)
5. Nathan Gerbe (Forward, Portland AHL)

CALGARY FLAMES:

The Flames have some interesting prospects at forward, who certainly have the size to stick at the NHL level. Mikael Backlund is a highly skilled, big Swedish center who could provide Jarome Iginla with a playmaking center. Greg Nemisz is a big winger who could learn a lot from watching Iginla play. Both of these players project to be top six forwards.

Unfortunately, the Flames don't look to have much in terms of top end defensive potential in their ranks. Tim Erixon could be a solid, second pairing two-way defenseman, and they have other players in that realm, but, especially since trading Dion Phaneuf, the Flames don't have much in terms of stud defenseman potential.

Calgary's Top Five:
1. Mikael Backlund (Forward, Abbotsford/Calgary AHL/NHL)
2. Greg Nemisz (Forward, Windsor OHL)
3. Tim Erixon (Defense, Skelleftea SEL)
4. Keith Seabrook (Defense, Abbotsford AHL)
5. T. J Brodie (Defense, Barrie OHL)

CAROLINA HURRICANES:

The Hurricanes have done a good job recently in strengthening their prospect ranks. Zach Boychuk, selected in the first round of 2008, looks to be a perfect complement to Eric Staal and Brandon Sutter at the center position. Moreover, Drayson Bowman looks to be a steal as a third round pick as his stock continues to rise as a top six winger.

However, their best pick could have been Jamie McBain in the second round of the 2006 draft. A very gifted offensive defenseman, McBain was a Hobey Baker award finalist at the University of Wisconsin-Madison and his offensive game translated well at the AHL level. It has been a tough season for Carolina, leading them to likely have a top 7 pick in the draft.

Possible First Round Targets:
1. Cam Fowler
2. Brandon Gormley
3. Brett Connolly/ Nino Niederreiter

Carolina's Top Five:
1. Jamie McBain (Defense, Albany AHL)
2. Zach Boychuk (Forward, Albany AHL)
3. Zac Dalpe (Forward, Ohio State NCAA)
4. Drayson Bowman (Forward, Albany AHL)
5. Brian Dumoulin (D, Boston College NCAA)

CHICAGO BLACKHAWKS:

The Blackhawks have benefited greatly from strong drafts. There team was built via great draft picks such as Jonathon Toews, Patrick Kane, Duncan Keith, and Brent Seabrook. However, it will be much more difficult this season with Blackhawks projecting to have a much lower pick then the top picks they had grown accustomed to before a season or two ago.

Their current prospect ranks include solid defensive prospects Dylan Olsen and Nick Leddy, both playing at the NCAA level and in need of development. In terms of forward prospects, they have Kyle Beach and Akim Aliu, two power forwards who are in need of adding discipline to their games. Jack Skille, a former top five pick, is pushing for a roster spot.

Possible First Round Targets:
1. Calvin Pickard
2. Beau Bennett

Chicago's Top Five:
1. Kyle Beach (Forward, Spokane WHL)
2. Nick Leddy (Defense, Minnesota NCAA)
3. Dylan Olsen (Defense, Minnesota-Duluth NCAA)
4. Jack Skille (Forward, Rockford AHL)
5. Akim Aliu (Forward, Rockford/Toledo

COLORADO AVALANCHE:

The Avalanche can credit much of their resurrection to extremely good drafting in recent years. Yes, Duchene was an obvious pick, but drafting Ryan O'Reilly in the second round could be considered one of the steals of the entire draft, as he immediately made the NHL squad.

In terms of their current prospect ranks, they have some nice defensive, top-line depth with Kevin Shattenkirk/Colby Cohen/Stefan Elliot. They also have a high character, big two-way center in Ryan Stoa. In terms of draft needs, the Avs could stand to take the best player available, but also need some help in depth on the wing or in net.

Possible First Round Targets:
1. Jack Campbell/Calvin Pickard
2. Tyler Toffoli
3. Quinton Howden

Colorado's Top Five:
1. Stefan Elliot (Defense, Saskatoon WHL)
2. Kevin Shattenkirk (Defense, Boston University NCAA)
3. Ryan Stoa (Forward, Lake Erie AHL)
4. Colby Cohen (Defense, Boston University NCAA)
5. Tyson Barrie (Defense, Kelowna WHL)

COLUMBUS BLUE JACKETS:

Obviously, the Nikita Filatov situation greatly affects the strength of the Blue Jackets system. After starting the season in North America, Filatov bolted to Russia when not happy with playing time.

If he comes back, Filatov is about as good as any prospect in hockey. Besides Filatov, the Blue Jackets have some solid defensive depth in Cody Goloubef and John Moore: solid two way defenseman with top four potential. After those two players, the Jackets lack top end talent, and need to upgrade their forward corps. With a likely top ten pick, the Jackets could stand to do so.

Possible First Round Targets
1. Eric Gudbranson
2. Brett Connolly
3. Cam Fowler

Columbus' Top Five:
1. Nikita Filatov (Forward, CSKA Moscow KHL)
2. Cody Goloubef (Defense, Wisconsin NCAA)
3. John Moore (Defense, Kitchener OHL)
4. Matt Clavert (Forward, Brandon WHL)
5. Maxim Mayorov (Forward, Syracuse AHL)

DALLAS STARS:

Sitting at the top of Dallas' prospect pool is first round pick and sniper Scott Glennie. However, the Stars have recently added some nice young skill to their lineup with the likes of Matt Niskanen, James Neal, and Loui Erikkson.

Still, with Mike Modano aging rapidly, Marty Turco on the way out and not enough depth on defense, the Stars need to use the draft to re-stock the cupboard. Specifically, it'd be nice to see them add a potential first line centerman or #1 goalie prospect.

Possible First Round Targets:
1. Jack Campbell
2. Jeff Skinner
3. Nick Bjugstad

Dallas' Top Five:
1. Scott Glennie (Forward, Brandon WHL)
.2. Alex Chiasson (Forward, Boston University NCAA)
3. Philip Larsen (Defense, Vastra Frolunda SEL)
4. Curtis McKenzie (Forward, Miami NCAA)
5. Perttu Lindgren (Forward, Texas AHL)

DETROIT RED WINGS:

The Red Wings always seem to have a steady stream of talent running through their organization and much of it comes from extremely smart drafting in every round.

Take for example, Gustav Nyquist, who just had a monster season for Maine in the NCAA and was taken by the Red Wings in the 4th round. Or, how about Brendan Smith, their first round pick in 2007 who is a finalist for the Hobey Baker Award.

The Wings don't exactly have many weak spots in their organization, but could stand to add some forward talent to their prospect ranks to complement the defensive players at the top in Smith and Jakub Kindl.

Possible First Round Targets:
1. Jaden Schwartz
2. Brad Ross
3. Dylan McIlrath

Red Wings' Top Five:
1. Brendan Smith (Defense, Wisconsin NCAA)
2. Jakub Kindle (Defense, Grand Rapids AHL)
3. Tomas Tatar (Forward, Grand Rapids AHL)
4. Gustav Nyquist (Forward, Maine NCAA)
5. Daniel Larsson (Goalie, Grand Rapids AHL)

EDMONTON OILERS:

Obviously, the past couple season's have not gone the way Edmonton would have liked. That said, they have none a rather nice job in the draft in acquiring some top end players with their early picks. Edmonton will have the #1 pick in this draft and they will be the center player in the Taylor vs. Tyler debate.

However, the Oilers all ready have a potential first line scoring winger in Magnus Paajarvi-Svensson, making Seguin a very good fit for the rebuilding team. In the end, they will be adding an elite talent this off-season.

Possible First Round Targets:
1. Tyler Seguin
2. Taylor Hall

Edmonton's Top Five:
1. Magnus Paajarvi-Svensson (Forward, Timra SEL)
2. Jordan Eberle (Forward, Regina/Springfield WHL/AHL)
3. Linus Omark (Forward, Moscow KHL)
4. Riley Nash (Forward, Cornell NCAA)
5. Alex Plante (Defense, Springfield AHL)

FLORIDA PANTHERS:

Florida has some very nice young talent playing for their NHL club right now. Players like David Booth, Michael Frolik, and Dimitry Kulikov have made smooth transitions to the NHL and look to be impact players for the Panthers for now and the future.

General Manager Randy Sexton made it clear that Florida wants to re-build, making this draft more important. However, with a goaltending prospect like Jacob Markstrom sitting at the top of their prospect ranks, they are heading in the right direction.

Possible First Round Targets:
1. Erik Gudbranson
2. Brett Connolly
3. Brandon Gormley
4. Cam Fowler

Florida's Top Five:
1. Jacob Markstrom (Goalie, Brynas SEL)
2. Alexander Salak (Goalie, Rochester AHL)
3. Keaton Ellerby (Defense, Rochester/Florida AHL/NHL)
4. Michael Repik (Forward, Rochester AHL)
5. Shawn Matthias (Forward, Rochester AHL)

LOS ANGELES KINGS:

After having several tough seasons, the Kings were able to draft well and add some young impact players to their squad. Obviously Drew Doughty is all ready one of the top defensemen in the league in just his second season, while Oscar Moller is just about ready for a full time NHL role.

The Kings strength is definitely in their defensive corps as they have a couple guys ready to join Doughty and co. They could stand to add some nice forward prospects to complement Anze Kopitar and Dustin Brown on the young, upstart Kings.

Possible First Round Targets:
1. Emerson Etem
2. Tyler Toffolli
3. Beau Bennett

Los Angeles' Top Five:
1. Brayden Schenn (Forward, Brandon WHL)
2. Thomas Hickey (Defense, Manchester AHL)
3. Colton Teubert (Defense, Regina WHL)
4. Jonathan Bernier (Goalie, Manchester AHL)
5. Jacob Muzzin (Defense, Soo OHL)

MINNESOTA WILD:

The Wild look like they will miss the playoffs again this season as they are struggling to take the next step in jumping from a fringe playoff team to a legitimate contender.

They recently traded their first round pick of 2009, Nick Leddy, to Chicago in exchange for NHL ready, smooth skating defenseman Cam Barker. This was fine, as the Wild still have some strong defensive prospects in the system, but need an infusion of exciting, young, offensive talent.

Possible First Round Targets:
1. Nick Bjugstad
2. Alexander Burmistrov
3. Derek Forbort

Minnesota's Top Five:
1. Marco Scandella (Defense, Val D'Or Foreurs QMJHL)
2. Tyler Cuma (Defense, Ottawa OHL)
3. Erik Haula (Forward, Omaha USHL)
4. Colton Gillies (Forward, Houston AHL)
5. Maxim Noreau (Defense, Houston AHL)

MONTREAL CANADIENS:

The Canadiens made a questionable trade, in shipping arguable top prospect Ryan McDonagh for Scott Gomez and his big salary, but they do have plenty of depth within their ranks to withstand that loss. The elevation of P.K Subban's game certainly helps.

They took hometown boy Louis Leblanc (who has actually spent the past two seasons playing in the United States) with their first rounder last season, and may want to look less into a project pick this year. They have relative equal depth at forward and defense.

Possible First Round Targets:
1. Alexander Burmistrov
2. Jeff Skinner
3. Mikael Granlund
4. Austin Watson

Montreal's Top Five:
1. P.K Subban (Defense, Hamilton AHL)
2. Louis Leblanc (Forward, Harvard NCAA)
3. Danny Kristo (Forward, North Dakota NCAA)
4. Aaron Palushaj (Forward, Hamilton AHL)
5. Yannick Weber (Defense, Hamilton AHL)

NASHVILLE PREDATORS:

It is clear the Predators have stocked their prospect cupboard with defense recently, and they have put themselves into a position to dominate on the back end with players like Shea Weber and Ryan Suter. However, they have also made some great value picks like NCAA sensation Blake Geoffrion and Alexander Sulzer (players taken later in the draft but look to have solid NHL potential). Despite having a future #1 or #2 center in Colin Wilson in the organization, the Predators could stand to add more offense in the draft.

Possible First Round Targets:
1. Brock Nelson
2. Emerson Etem
3. Tyler Toffoli

Nashville's Top Five:
1. Jon Blum (Defense, Milwaukee AHL)
2. Colin Wilson (Forward Milwaukee AHL)
3. Ryan Ellis (Defense, Windsor OHL)
4. Charles Olivier-Roussel (Defense, Shawnigan QMJHL)
5. Zach Budish (Forward, Minnesota NCAA)

NEW JERSEY DEVILS:

There is a reason the Devils never seem to get worse, and it's because they take advantage of their picks. Zach Parise, Travis Zajac and Paul Martin were all either lower first round or high second round draft picks that are now pivotal players on their squad.

Now, considering they traded one of their top prospects and first round pick this season for Kovalchuk, they will have to hope they can hit in the lower second round again this season. Obviously, as they have no first round, we won't label those targets.

In terms of their current prospects, Mattias Tedenby can just watch Zach Parise play to realize what he can become and Jacob Josefson could be a solid two-way, top six center for the organization. They also potentially have a Brodeur replacement in former Gopher goalie Jeff Frazee.

New Jersey's Top Five:
1. Mattias Tedenby (Forward, HV71 SEL)
2. Jacob Josefson (Forward, Djuragardens SEL)
3. Alexander Urbom (Defense, Brandon WHL)
4. Nick Palmieri (Defense, Lowell AHL)
5. Jeff Frazee (Goalie, Lowell AHL)

NEW YORK ISLANDERS:

After multiple subpar seasons, the Islanders showed signs of life this season before fading and guaranteeing themselves a high draft pick yet again. Last year's number one overall pick John Tavares made a smooth transition and could have a Stamkos-esque explosion next season, while other young players such as Josh Bailey and Kyle Okposo are proving themselves to be players to build around as the Islanders continue to re-build.

Rob Schremp, sent back and forth by Edmonton to hockey purgatory, has caught on well with the Islanders. With this draft, HockeyProspect would like to see the Islanders improve their young defensive corps.

Possible First Round Targets:
1. Eric Gudbranson
2. Brandon Gormley
3. Cam Fowler:

New York's Top Five:
1. Travis Harmonic (Defense, Brandon WHL)
2. Calvin de Haan (Defense, Oshawa OHL)
3. Kirill Petrov (Forward, Kazan KHL)
4. Rhett Rakhshani (Forward, Denver NCAA)
5. Trevor Smith (Forward, Bridgeport AHL)

NEW YORK RANGERS:

The Rangers look to have taken one of the steals of the 2009 draft by taking Chris Kreider, currently playing for Boston College. They also took his USA World Junior Championship teammate Derek Stepan in the 2nd round of the 2008 draft, and both look to be top prospects in all of hockey.

Recent graduate Artem Anisimov has looked good in his rookie season and everyone knows about the success of Michael Del Zotto in his rookie campaign. Overall, the Rangers have some nice depth and look to developing a solid young core.

Possible First Round Targets:
1. Derek Forbort
2. Ryan Johansen
3. Nino Niederreiter

New York's Top Five:
1. Evgeny Grachev (Forward, Hartford AHL)
2. Chris Kreider (Forward, Boston College NCAA)
3. Derek Stepan (Forward, Wisconsin NCAA)
4. Ryan McDonagh (Defense, Wisconsin NCAA)
5. Bobby Sanguinetti (Defense, Hartford AHL)

OTTAWA SENATORS:

Going into this season you could argue that the Senators desperately needed to find a goalie of the future in this season's draft. However, Brian Elliott seems to have taken the reigns there and is worth reyling on.

The Senators have drafted defensemen well, with Erik Karlsson already contributing and big-bodied Jared Cowen ready to step in shortly. They also recently signed NCAA free agents Bobby Butler and Patrick Wiercioch to add depth to their system. However, their forward prospects leave a lot to be desired and should be what they address with their first round pick.

Possible First Round Targets
1. Ryan Johansen
2. Emerson Etem
3. Tyler Toffoli

Ottawa's Top Five:
1. Jared Cowen (Defense, Spokane WHL)
2. Louie Caporusso (Forward, Michigan NCAA)
3. Patrick Wiercioch (Defense, Denver, NCAA)
4. Andre Peterrson (Forward, HV71 SEL)
5. Ilya Zubov (Forward, Binghamton AHL)

PHILADELPHIA FLYERS:

The Flyers were able to draft very well in the first round of 2007 and 2008, grabbing Claude Giroux and James Van Riemsdyk, both contributing to the NHL squad already. However, they simply haven't made enough of their first round picks and don't have one this season or next.

They traded 2008 pick Luca Sbisa and their 2009/2010 firsts for Chris Pronger, making it very difficult for them to maintain organizational depth. If it weren't for Giroux and Van Riemsdyk translating well to the NHL game, they could be in trouble. The Flyers need to hope that Eriksson can translate to a true NHL goalie as well.

Philadelphia's Top Five:
1. Ville Leino (Forward, Detroit/Philadelphia NHL)
2. Joacim Eriksson (Goalie, Brynas SEL)
3. Marc-Andre Bourdon (Defense, Adirondack AHL)
4. Kevin Marshall (Defense, Adirondack AHL)
5. Patrick Maroon (Forward, Adirondack AHL)

PHOENIX COYOTES:

Easily the best story of the NHL this season, the Coyotes' draft picks are really starting to pay off with players like Keith Yandle contributing greatly to their resurgence.

However, the Coyotes look to get even stronger as they have some serious front end talent playing in the AHL and juniors right now. They also have a potential stud defenseman in 2009 first round pick Oliver Ekman-Larsson. They look to have a late first round pick in this year's draft, and should target defensemen, but may have to settle on a forward.

Possible First Round Targets: (2 picks)
1. Mark Pysyk
2. Jaden Schwartz
1. Jon Merrill
2. Tyler Pitlick

Phoenix's Top Five:
1. Kyle Turris (Forward, San Antonio AHL)
2. Oliver Ekman-Larsson (Defense, Leksands SEL)
3. Michael Boedker (Forward, San Antonio AHL)
4. Brett MacLean (Forward, San Antonio AHL)
5. Viktor Tikhonov (Forward, Cherepovets KHL)

PITTSBURGH PENGUINS:

Obviously, the core of the Penguins was essentially handed to them with top draft picks in Sidney Crosby, Evgeni Malkin, Jordan Staal, and goaltender Marc-Andre Fleury. However, other key components to their squad such as Brooks Orpik and Kris Letang were taken with a low first round and third round, respectively.

So, clearly, the Penguins have taken advantage of their drafts. Per usual in the past couple seasons, the Penguins look to have a very low first round pick this season. Their top prospect, Eric Tangradi was acquired in a trade and could end up being a dominant power forward in the NHL. We think they could use some defensive depth in their system.

Possible First Round Targets:
1. Dylan McIlrath
2. Stanislav Galiev
3. Jon Merrill

Pittsburgh's Top Five:
1. Eric Tangradi (Forward, Wilkes-Barre, AHL)
2. Simon Despres (Defense, Saint John QMJHL)
3. Carl Sneep (Defense, Boston College NCAA)
4. Dustin Jeffrey (Forward, Wilkes-Barre AHL)
5. Ben Hanowski (Forward, St. Cloud NCAA)

SAN JOSE SHARKS:

Annually a top team in the NHL, the Sharks have not been blessed with high first round picks to easily stabilize their system. However, with lower picks they have made great additions to their team with players such as Joe Pavelski (7th round pick), Ryan Clowe (6th round pick), and Marc-Edouard Vlasic (2nd round pick).

Still to take the next step to a Stanley Cup contender, the Sharks must hope that their young prospects are players with good winning intangibles and can play multiple roles, as their first line is essentially set for years to come.

Possible First Round Targets:
1. Dylan McIlrath
2. Brock Nelson
3. Beau Bennett

San Jose's Top Five:
1. Logan Couture (Forward, Worcester/San Jose, AHL/NHL)
2. Nick Petrecki (Defense, Worcester, AHL)
3. James Marcou (Forward, UMASS, NCAA)
4. Alex Stalock (Goalie, Worcester, AHL)
5. Jason Demers (Defense, Worcester/San Jose, AHL/NHL)

ST. LOUIS BLUES:

The Blues have been known as one of the top drafting teams in recent years; acquiring young players that have been able to step into the league quickly such as Erik Johnson, T.J Oshie, Patrick Berglund and David Backes.

However, they also have studs such as Alex Pietrangelo (widely considered one of the best drafted players not in the NHL) and Lars Eller, ready to join the NHL ranks soon. One thing the Blues seem to be missing is goaltending depth, and that could be a target of theirs come draft day.

Possible First Round Targets:
1. Jack Campbell
2. Alexander Burmistrov
3. Austin Watson

St. Louis' Top Five:
1. Alex Pietrangelo (Defense, Barrie, OHL)
2. Lars Eller (Forward, Peoria, AHL)
3. David Rundblad (Defense, Skelleftea, SEL)
4. Ian Cole (Defense, Notre Dame/Peoria, NCAA/AHL)
5. Jake Allen (Goalie, Drummondville QMJHL)

TAMPA BAY LIGHTNING:

With their first pick in 2008 (#1 overall), the Lightning chose their forward of the future with Steven Stamkos. In 2009, with the second overall pick, they followed suit with their defenseman of the future: Victor Hedman.

So far, both picks have worked out great and the Lightning seem to be on the cusp of breaking into a perennial playoff contender. They could certainly use some more defensive depth in their prospect ranks, but with their top pick looking to be top seven or so, should again go with the best player available.

Possible First Round Targets:
1. Brandon Gormley
2. Brett Connolly
3. Nino Niederreiter

Tampa Bay's Top Five:
1. Dustin Tokarski (Goalie, Norfolk AHL)
2. Carter Ashton (Forward, Lethbridge/Regina, WHL)
3. Dana Tyrell (Forward, Norfolk , AHL)
4. Ty Wishart (Defense, Norfolk, AHL)
5. Richard Panik (Forward, Norfolk, AHL)

TORONTO MAPLE LEAFS:

We all know the current situation with Toronto. Brash General Manager Brian Burke has his own version of rebuilding which led to him trading away his 2009-2010 first pick and 2010-2011 first along with a second round pick for Phil Kessel.

We don't think Brian expected the Maple Leafs pick would be a top two pick, and thus have them miss out on a franchise player. Still, Burke has worked hard to put a product on the ice that will improve and in making moves for a players like Kessel and then Dion Phaneuf, he might just do so. College player signees such as Tyler Bozak and Christian Hanson look to be decent pro prospects.

Toronto's Top Five:
1. Nazem Kadri (Forward, London OHL)
2. Keith Aulie (Defense, Toronto AHL)
3. Chris DiDomenico (Forward, Drummondville QMJHL)
4. Jerry D'Amigo (Forward, RPI NCAA)
5. Jimmy Hayes (Forward, Boston College NCAA)

VANCOUVER CANUCKS:

The Canucks, despite consistently being a playoff team, have a great prospect system. They have serious forward talents in the prospect system, and picks such as Alex Edler and Ryan Kesler have contributed well to the NHL club.

Obviously, they have some top end forwards in the system with Cody Hodgson and a potential #1 goalie in Cory Schneider. They could stand to add some defensive depth to their system with their low first round pick.

Possible First Round Targets:
1. Dylan McIlrath
2. Jon Merrill
3. Steven Johns

Vancouver's Top Five:
1. Cody Hodgson (Forward, Brampton, OHL)
2. Cory Schneider (Goalie, Manitoba, AHL)
3. Jordan Schroeder (Forward, Minnesota, NCAA)
4. Michael Grabner (Forward, Manitoba, AHL)
5. Sergei Shirokov (Forward, Manitoba, AHL)

WASHINGTON CAPITALS:

The Capitals, despite having one of the more star studded lineups in the NHL, have done well to draft players that can fill roles with a first line that is all but locked up for years to come.

What the Caps seem to lack in their organization is two-way forwards and shut down defenseman. John Carlson is a lock to be a high end player in the league for years.

Out guess is that the Caps will probably take the best player available when they are on the clock in round one.

Possible First Round Targets:
1. Maxim Kitsyn
2. Dylan McIlrath
3. Brock Nelson

Washington's Top Five:
1. John Carlson (Defense, Hershey, AHL)
2. Karl Alzner (Defense, Hershey, AHL)
3. Marcus Johansson (Forward, Farjestads, SEL)
4. Andrew Gordon (Forward, Hershey, AHL)
5. Francois Bouchard (Forward, Hershey, AHL)

4

PLAYER RANKINGS
2010 NHL DRAFT

ROUND 1

1	Tyler Seguin	Plymouth OHL
2	Taylor Hall	Windsor OHL
3	Erik Gudbranson	Kingston OHL
4	Brett Connolly	Prince George WHL
5	Cam Fowler	Windsor OHL
6	Vladimir Tarasenko	Novosibirsk Siber KHL
7	Brandon Gormley	Moncton QMJHL
8	Alexander Burmistrov	Barrie OHL
9	Nino Niederreiter	Portland WHL
10	Nick Bjugstad	HS USA
11	Jeff Skinner	Kitchener OHL
12	Mikael Granlund	Karpat FIN
13	Jack Campbell (G)	U-18 USHL
14	Jaden Schwartz	TriCity USHL
15	Mark Pysyk	Edmonton WHL
16	Derek Forbort	U-18 USHL
17	Ryan Johansen	Portland WHL
18	Emerson Etem	Medicine Hat WHL
19	Austin Watson	Peterborough OHL
20	Tyler Toffoli	Ottawa OHL
21	Dylan McIlrath	Moose Jaw WHL
22	Riley Sheahan	NotreDame NCAA
23	Brock Nelson	Warroad HS
24	Quinton Howden	Moose Jaw WHL
25	Tyler Pitlick	Minnesota St - Mankato
26	Maxim Kitsyn	Magnitogorsk KHL
27	Stanislav Galiev	St.John QMJHL
28	Jon Merrill	U-18 USHL
29	Beau Bennett	Penticton Vees BCHL
30	Steven Johns	U-18 USHL

ROUND 2

31	Jared Tinordi	U-18 USHL
32	Greg McKegg	Erie OHL
33	Tom Kuhnhackl	Landshut GER
34	Jordan Weal	Regina WHL
35	Brad Ross	Portland WHL
36	Alex Petrovic	Red Deer WHL
37	Jared Knight	London OHL
38	Joey Hishon	Owen Sound OHL
39	John McFarland	Sudbury OHL
40	Kirill Kabanov	Moncton QMJHL
41	Kevin Hayes	Noble Greenough Prep
42	Calvin Pickard (G)	Seattle WHL
43	Brooks Macek	Tri-City WHL
44	Ryan Spooner	Peterborough OHL
45	Ivan Telegin	Sagiaw OHL
46	Charlie Coyle	South Shore EJHL
47	Petr Straka	Rimouski QMJHL
48	Troy Rutkowski	Portland WHL
49	Curtis Hamilton	Saskatoon WHL
50	Andrew Yogan	Erie OHL
51	Ryan Martindale	Ottawa OHL
52	Sam Brittain (G)	Canmore AJHL
53	Yasin Cisse	Des Moines USHL
54	Steven Silas	Belleville OHL
55	Jerome Gauthier-Leduc	Rouyn-Noranda
56	Brian Billett (G)	Jr. Monarchs EJHL
57	Sam Carrick	Brampton OHL
58	Kent Simpson (G)	Everett WHL
59	Jakub Culek	Rimouski QMJHL
60	Petr Mrazek (G)	Ottawa OHL

ROUND 3

61	Mark Visentin (G)	Niagara OHL
62	Teemu Pulkkinen	Jokerit FIN
63	Evgeny Kuznetsov	Chelyabinsk RUS
64	Max Gardiner	HS USA
65	Justin Faulk	U-18 USHL
66	Calle Jarnkrok	Sweden Jr.
67	Geoffrey Schemitsch	Owen Sound OHL
68	Austin Madaisky	Kamloops WHL
69	Matthew Bissonnette	Lewiston QMJHL
70	Jonathan Johansson	Sweden
71	Samuel Carrier	Lewiston QMJHL
72	Devante Smith-Pelly	Mississauga OHL
73	Steven Shipley	Owen Sound OHL
74	Oscar Lindberg	SKELLEFTEA JR.
75	Dalton Smith	Ottawa OHL
76	Jason Zucker	U-18 USHL
77	Louis Domingue (G)	Quebec
78	Michael Bournival	Shawinigan QMJHL
79	Trevor Parkes	Montreal QMJHL
80	Bill Arnold	U-18 USHL
81	Johan Alm	Sweden
82	Louis-Marc Aubry	Montreal QMJHL
83	Mark Stone	Brandon WHL
84	Luke Moffatt	U-18 USHL
85	Brock Beukeboom	Sault Ste. Marie OHL
86	Dannick Gauthier	St.John QMJHL
87	Kevin Sundher	Chilliwack WHL
88	Cameron Wind	Brampton OHL
89	Jonas Gunnarsson (G)	HV 71 JR. SWE
90	Austin Levi	Plymouth OHL

ROUND 4

91	Brandon Archibald	Sault Ste. Marie OHL
92	Zane Gothberg (G)	Thief River Falls
93	Janos Hari	Färjestad J18
94	Mathieu Corbeil (G)	Halifax
95	Kevin Gravel	Sioux City USHL
96	Jason Clark	Shattuck
97	Danny Biega	Harvard NCAA
98	Josh Shalla	Saginaw OHL
99	Jonathan Parker	Seattle WHL
100	Connor Brickley	Des Moines USHL
101	Christian Thomas	Oshawa OHL
102	Michael Chaput	Lewiston QMJHL
103	Nathan Chiarlitti	Sarnia OHL
104	Morgan Ellis	Cape Breton
105	Joe Rogalski	Sarnia OHL
106	Alexei Marchenko	CSKA Moscow
107	Mark Alt	Cretin-Derham
108	Sami Aittokallio (G)	Ilves Jr FIN
109	Victor Öhman	Sweden
110	Kevin Lind	Chicago Steel
111	Justin Holl	Minnetonka
112	Antonin Honejsek	Moose Jaw WHL
113	Brandon Davidson	Regina WHL
114	Daniel Gunnarsson	Sweden Leksand Jr.
115	Sergei Barbashev	CSKA Moscow
116	Martin Marincin	Slovakia
117	Joe Basaraba	Shattuck
118	Brett Bulmer	Kelowna WHL
119	Scott Wedgewood (G)	Plymouth OHL
120	Alex Emond	Rimouski QMJHL

ROUND 5

121	Philipp Grubauer (G)	Belleville OHL
122	Michael MacDonald	London OHL
123	Jordan Messier	Tri-City OHL
124	Pavel Kulikov	Reaktor
125	Reid McNeill	London OHL
126	Michael Houser (G)	London OHL
127	Phil Lane	Brampton OHL
128	Julian Melchiori	Newmarket (CCHL)
129	Jonathan Brunelle	Drummondville QMJHL
130	Nick Czinder	Youngstown USHL
131	Freddie Hamilton	Niagara OHL
132	Martin Ouellette (G)	Kimball Union Academy
133	Jacob Fallon	Indiana USHL
134	Craig Cunningham	Vancouver WHL
135	Aaron Harstad	Green Bay USHL
136	Brandon Hynes	Victoriaville QMJHL
137	Matt White	Pittsburgh Midget AAA
138	Ludvig Rensfeldt	Brynas Jr.Sweden
139	Kendall McFaull	Moose Jaw WHL
140	Patrik Nemeth	Aik Sweden Jr
141	Joakim Nordsrom	Sweden Jr.
142	Etienne Boutet	Rimouski QMJHL
143	Tomas Filippi	Liberc Jr.
144	Johan Larsson	Brynas Jr.Sweden
145	Darren Archibald	Barrie OHL
146	Colin Campbell	Vaughan OJAHL
147	Justin Shugg	Windsor OHL
148	Stephen Macauly	St.John QMJHL
149	Michael Pereira	Avon Old Farms
150	JP. Anderson (G)	Mississauga OHL

ROUND 6

151	Charles Inglis	Saskatoon WHL
152	Alex Guptill	Orangeville CCHL
153	Luke Curadi	Penticton BCHL
154	Brandon Foote (G)	Guelph OHL
155	Matt Mackenzie	Calgary WHL
156	Alain Berger	Oshawa OHL
157	Maxime Clermont (G)	Gatineau QMJHL
158	Josh Nicholls	Saskatoon WHL
159	Riley Brace	Mississauga OHL
160	Nikita Zaytsev	Sibir Novosibirsk
161	Nikita Gusev	CSKA-Red Army
162	Pat McNally	Milton Academy
163	Kenneth Agostino	Delbarton
164	Spencer Asuchak	Prince George WHL
165	Blake Gal	Spokane WHL
166	Adam Petterson	Sweden
167	David Mazurek	Barrie Colts
168	Brendan Gallagher	Vancouver WHL
169	Artem Voronin	Spartak Moscow
170	Taylor Carnevale	Barrie OHL
171	Andrew Shaw	Niagara OHL
172	Nick Mattson	Indiana USHL
173	Willie Yanakeff (G)	Sioux City USHL
174	Brandon Alderson	Sarnia OHL
175	Nick Trecapelli	Sudbury OHL
176	Mathieu Brisson	Omaha USHL
177	Dylen McKinlay	Chilliwack WHL
178	Chris Wagner	South Shore EJHL
179	Alex Theriau	Everett WHL
180	Ryan O'Connor	Saginaw OHL

ROUND 7

181	Benjamin Conz (G)	Langnau
182	Taylor Aronson	Portland WHL
183	Andrew Crescenzi	Kitchener OHL
184	Clay Witt (G)	Sioux Falls USHL
185	Greg Sutch	Mississauga OHL
186	Alex Micallef	Villanova OJAHL
187	JT Barnett	Vancouver WHL
188	Adam Sedlak	Peterborough OHL
189	Jani Hakanpaa	Finland Jr.
190	Ignat Zemchenko	Almaz Russia
191	Bryan Rust	U-18 USHL
192	Brendan Woods	Chicago USHL
193	Casey Thrush	Maryland Mid AAA
194	Colin MacDonald	Plymouth OHL
195	Patrick Geering	Zurich
196	Tyler Stahl	Chilliwack WHL
197	Colby Drost (G)	Holderness (H.S)
198	Matt Petgrave	Niagara OHL
199	Max Reinhart	Kootenay WHL
200	Steven Beyers	Orangeville CCHL
201	Justin Dowling	Swift Current WHL
202	Brendan Ranford	Kamloops WHL
203	Guillaume Asselin	Montreal QMJHL
204	Ryan Daugherty	Omaha USHL
205	Chris Desousa	London OHL
206	Justin Feser	Tri-City OHL
207	Nick Sorkin	Waterloo USHL
208	Mike Reardon	Noble & Greenough
209	Jay Gilbert	Plymouth OHL
210	Scott Wamsganz	Waterloo USHL

5

2011 NHL Draft Prospects

Adam Larsson

Defense - Skellefteå AIK
Born November 12, 1992 Skellefteå, Swe
Height 6.02 Weight 210 Shoots Right

Well we just loved Victor Hedman, so dare we say that Larsson is better? The jury is still out but he is a player who is truly making a name for himself and has a chance to be the first overall pick in the 2011 NHL Draft.

Larsson blows us away with the maturity he plays with at such a young age. On most nights you would never be able to guess that he is a 16 year old rookie.

He is an excellent skater, has a great shot and makes fantastic reads all over the ice. He has great vision and elite hockey sense. Adam is 6'2" and weighs in at 210 pounds. He can go multiple games without making a mental mistake. It's very impressive to say the least. Did we mention he is playing with men?

Sean Couturier

Left Wing - Drummondville (OHL)
Born Dec 7 1992 Bathurst, NB
Height 6.03 Weight 185 Shoots L

All Couturier did was win the QMJHL scoring title at age 17, a year before his NHL draft year. The Bathurst native racked up 41 goals and added 55 assists in just his second QMJHL season.

As a prospect he does it all. When he enters the offensive zone he really dictates the play. It is scary for opposing teams to see Sean hop the boards for each shift. Sean is a big lanky kid who can really handle the puck. He looks much older than a 17 year old the way he can be so dominant on so many shifts.

He has all the tools. He can shoot with authority, is a terrific playmaker and he knows how to use his body.

We love the long reach that he seems to utilize often. We can't wait to see what he can do as he matures more physically over the summer and enters into a battle with Swedish defenseman, Adam Larsson and possibly WHL star Ryan Nugent Hopkins for the #1 overall spot in June 2011.

Ryan Nugent Hopkins

Center - Red Deer (WHL)
Born Apr 12 1993 Burnaby, BC
Height 6.00 Weight 155 Shoots L

The Burnaby native was the 1st overall selection in the WHL draft by the Rebels. He entered his rookie year with plenty of expectations and he has delivered. The rookie posted 24 goals and 41 helpers to get him off and running as he heads into his NHL draft season next fall.

In some other NHL drafts, Ryan would have had a great shot at being the top pick. Unfortunately he has players named Larsson and Couturier who will battle him for that honor next season.

Ryan has great puck skills and is clearly a smart hockey player. It is easy to forget how young he is, when you see the maturity on the ice. His skating needs to improve a bit, but it's not holding him back at the WHL level. He is a very creative playmaker and a flat out fun player to watch.

Nugent-Hopkins will need a good off season program to help him fill out and build up some strength before his draft year begins.

Ryan Murphy

Defense - Kitchener (OHL)
Born Mar 31 1993 Aurora, ONT
Height 5.10 Weight 160 Shoots R

He is worth the price of admission. He has amazingly quick feet that give him so much mobility in all situations. Murphy is one of those players that makes guys around him better. Watching him carry the puck up ice as he surveys the passing options is a pleasure to watch.

He has come miles in his own end in just one year under head coach Steve Spott and his staff. There were times watching him play for his Minor Midget York Simcoe team where he was overmatched on the walls. It concerned us a bit heading to the OHL against the bigger stronger players. He needs to keep improving but it's not like he is losing ice time for defensive concerns.

In the offensive zone he really shows his skills. Murphy uses those quick feet and great vision to help QB a power play. He unloads his slap shot very quickly and it's accurate.

We expect big numbers from him in 2010/2011.

Boone Jenner

Center - Oshawa (OHL)
Born Jun 15 1993 Dorchester, ONT
Height 6.01 Weight 193 Shoots L

Boone Jenner has good size at 6'1", 193 lbs and uses it to his advantage, protecting the puck very well. He had a great rookie season in the OHL and if a player named Matt Puempel didn't exist, he would have been the talk of all OHL rookies.

Jenner is a goal scorer and an excellent passer. His playmaking skills this season may have even exceeded expectations. He has good speed and a pretty good head for the game, with very good overall upside. He is very skilled with the puck, and is a very dangerous player. Boone is impressive with the puck with great speed off the rush.

Oshawa should be an improved team which can't do anything but help Boone heading into an important season for him. Jenner had a great rookie season and has placed himself in a good position heading into his NHL Draft year.

Scott Harrington

Defense - London (OHL)
Born Mar 10 1993 Kingston, ONT
Height 6.01 Weight 190 Shoots L

We have watched this kid a lot over the last two seasons. We first saw him playing up a year with the 1992's in the OHL Cup. He impressed in his Minor Midget season playing good smart hocket all season long. Scott then finished the season in Junior 'A' with Kingston, where he went all the way to the Royal Bank Cup. London stole him with their first round pick and he has logged a ton of ice time all year long.

Harrington plays with the poise of a veteran, as he seems to make all the right decisions with the puck. He reads the game so well that it lets him anticipate the play and make plays all over the ice. He has been doing a great job of knowing when to jump into the rush. The Hunters have no problem activating their d-men and Harrington is really starting to implement it into his game.

London surprised some folks this year. Given the return of players like Knight, DeSousa, McDonald, D'Orazio and Erlich, Harrington will have a good supporting cast in his NHL draft season.

Gabriel Landeskog

Right Wing - Kitchener (OHL)
Born Nov 23 1992 Stockholm, Sweden
Height 6.00 Weight 201 Shoots L

Landeskog is a HockeyProspect.com favorite. This kid might surprise some scouts when they start watching him more closely next season. The late 92 birth date makes 2011 his NHL draft year and Gabriel can flat out play. He is a very solid hockey player in just about every facet. He is a player coaches love to have on their teams because he is so smart and can be trusted in any situation.

Landeskog buried 24 chances this season as an OHL rookie and chipped in with another 22 assists. In a recent playoff game versus Saginaw his hustle on defense was outstanding and a great example of what he brings on a game by game basis. He chases down and wins loose pucks. His effort applying back pressure is outstanding.

We are guessing that Jeff Skinner will not quite crack the NHL next season. Watch out for the Rangers next year when the OHL will be Memorial Cup hosts. With Skinner, Murphy and Landeskog returning it is a nice base to build from.

Garrett Meurs

Center - Plymouth Whalers
Born Jan 12 1993 Ripley, ONT
Height 5.11 Weight 170 Shoots R

We were big fans of Meurs coming out of Minor Midget. Meurs is a player who is flying under the radar a little bit down in Plymouth but had a great rookie season.

Meurs has the potential to develop into a very productive NHL player.. His puck control, shooting and overall play making abilities are fantastic. His skating is improved and he seems to have an extra gear with the puck.

Meurs defensive game was a weak spot heading into his OHL rookie season. It's improved after a full season but will still need to get better. His offensive talent lets him slide a bit, but his draft stock will need defense in his game for him to stay up in the rankings.

He is fun to watch at top speed because he thinks fast and is a very capable playmaker. Having said that, goal scoring seems to be natural to him and is his bread and butter.

Vincent Trocheck

Center - Saginaw Spirit
Born Jul 11 1993 Pittsburgh, PA
Height 5.10 Weight 165 Shoots R

Trocheck is another player who might be slightly under the radar like Meurs, because he plays his hockey south of the border in Saginaw.

We really like this kid's potential. He looks much bigger than his listed height of 5'10" that was posted in September. If he gets a bit bigger and stronger, he should be able to become a player at the next level.

He is a goal scorer with a hard and accurate shot and has sniper written all over him. He is not overly physical but he does not shy away either. He does a great job at reading the play and makes good decisions off the rush.

Our biggest surprise was his compete level on defense. For a rookie, he was pretty impressive with his level of play in his own zone and through the neutral zone as he angled and fore-checked.

A prospect to watch as next season gets rolling.

Zach Hall

Center – Couchiching (OJAHL)
Born Apr 29 1993 Belleville, ONT
Height 5.11 Weight 166 Shoots L

We didn't want to just throw the top ten 2011 draft prospects at you in this section of the book. While we have obviously mentioned some high end and well known players, we also wanted to tell you about a few players who might start out being down the rankings in some of the pre-season NHL draft lists.

Zach Hall blew us away leading up to the OHL Draft in 2009. He is an elite playmaker and scorer, who works his tail off shift after shift. If not for a powerhouse Barrie team, he would have played in the OHL all season. He did chip in with a goal and an assist with limited ice in 5 games with the Colts.

Hall played Junior 'A' for the Couchiching Terriers and finished second on his team in scoring behind former OHL 1st rounder Matt Smyth. Hall's numbers were sick for a rookie: 71 pts in 44 games, including 26 goals. He will get plenty of ice time next season in Barrie. His slight build needs to improve.

Ty Rattie

Right Wing - Portland (WHL)
Born Feb 5 1993 Airdrie, ALTA
Height 6.00 Weight 167 Shoots R

As the 2nd overall pick behind Red Deer's Ryan Nugent-Hopkins in the 2008 WHL Bantam draft, Rattie got his chance to join the WHL full-time this season. Rattie managed 17 goals and 20 assists in a solid rookie campaign.

Rattie has outstanding goal scoring instincts and excellent hockey smarts. He is one of the hardest workers on every shift and is at his best when he has the puck.

Rattie needs to improve his game without the puck and learn to distribute the puck a bit better. If you speak to former coaches, they will tell you about his work ethic and his focus as a player. Rattie is wise beyond his years.

Rattie features a very good shot and is not afraid to use it. Portland has a solid core of 1992's and a very good 1993 in Ty Rattie.

Tyler Biggs

Right Wing – USA NTDP (USHL)
Born Apr 30 1993 Cincinnati, OH
Height 6.02 Weight 200

We know him well, as he played on one of our prospect teams and was also coached by a colleague of HP.

Biggs makes good use of his great speed. He can really move for a big power forward. He has had a good rookie year in the NTDP and committed to Miami much to the chagrin of Chris Dipiero and the Oshawa Generals.

Biggs enjoyed a great holiday season, beating some former teammates as Team USA beat Canada in the gold medal final of the Under-17. Biggs had a great tournament and a better final. Biggs showed both sides of his game in that one game. He can bury the puck and he can crash and bang. He uses his size well to win pucks. His scoring touch continues to improve.

Biggs is a hard worker and should be an absolutely huge physical specimen by the time his NHL draft day arrives next June.

Duncan Siemens

Defense - Saskatoon (WHL)
Born Sept 11 1993 Sherwood Park, AB
Height 6.03 Weight 192 Shoots L

Siemens was the first defenseman taken and the 3rd player taken overall in the 2008 WHL Bantam Draft. Duncan got stronger and stronger as the season progressed, finishing with 3 goals, 17 assists for 20 points to go along with 89 penalty minutes and a modest +11 rating.

Siemens already has NHL size. Siemens is a very confident puck handler and makes a terrific outlet pass. Duncan showed tremendous offensive instincts, by picking his spots and carrying the puck up ice late in the season for scoring chances. As the season progressed, Duncan began to see some power play time and didn't disappoint. He shows good reads in the offensive zone. Siemens also does a good job with an active stick as well.

There are not too many holes in Siemens game, but if one were to get picky he could work on his confidence, because he has even more to give. Siemens is a sure fire 2011 NHL first rounder and compares favorably to World Junior Defenseman Colten Teubert with more offensive upside.

David Musil

Defense - Vancouver (WHL)
Born April 9 1993 Delta (BC)
Height 6.03 Weight 191 Shoots L

Hockey is definitely in the blood of David Musil. His father, Frank Musil was a long time NHL'er. Musil had an outstanding 16 year old season in the WHL, accumulating 7 goals and 25 assists for 32 points. Musil was also an eye popping +33 for the Vancouver Giants.

Musil positions himself extremely well, and has great hockey sense in all aspects of the game. His raw offensive tools are top notch in terms of finding team mates on the power play. His biggest attribute is his size and how affectively he uses it to his advantage in all situations to separate defenders from the puck.

Musil could stand to improve on his skating. In addition, he could work on his shot and getting it off a bit quicker. He seemed to get better though as the season progressed which is a good sign.

Musil has drawn comparisons to Victor Hedman and could be one of the better Czech Prospects in recent memory. It is very possible that David Musil will be a top 5 draft pick in 2011.

Shane McColgan

Right Wing - Kelowna (WHL)
Born January 1 1993 Man. Beach, CA
Height 5.10 Weight 170 Shoots R

McColgan is another in what is getting to be a very long line of talented Californians entering the WHL. His rookie season didn't disappoint fans after all the hype surrounding the young American before entering the dub. McColgan finished with outstanding offensive totals for a 16 year old in the rough and tumble WHL, notching 25 goals and 44 assists for 69 points.

McColgan has great hands and is an above average skater. He is very illusive weaving into the offensive zone before slowing down and surveying the layout of his team mates like a surgeon. He has a very good snap shot and combines all these offensive tools with a bit of a temper and attitude similar to a Steve Downie (without the suspension antics). Once he enters the offensive zone, his vision is high end and leaves fans shaking their heads with the precision he shows on his passes.

Shane could improve on his defensive zone play. He sometimes won't get as dirty along the boards in his own end as he will in the offensive zone. If he can improve in this area, Shane won't see himself in junior for much more than a year or two. He definitely plays in the right system to work on this in Kelowna.

McColgan is one of the top 1993 born prospects in the USA and quite easily the top American born prospect in the Western USA. Look for Shane to garner a look in the first round of the 2011 NHL Draft.

Jesse Forsberg
Defense- Prince George (WHL)
Born August 13 1993 Waldheim, SK
Height 6.00 Weight 194 Shoots L

Forsberg was drafted 11th overall in the 2008 WHL Bantam Draft and was the top defenseman taken from Saskatchewan in his draft season. He has parlayed his bantam success and high draft ranking into a successful year in Midget last season and fantastic 16 year old season in the WHL.

This season was a trying one for the Prince George Cougars of the WHL, but one of the lone bright spots this year was undoubtedly Jesse Forsberg. He put up 1 goal and 15 assists and was a -19 which sounds bad but was one of the best on his team. Forsberg had 103 penalty minutes.

Forsberg is very tenacious on the boards and hates losing any battle. He is already able to weave out of his own zone with confidence, which is a good sign at his age and even more so given the lack of help he had this season. Forsberg will mix it up and doesn't back down from a challenge. He is very vocal on the ice already and took on somewhat of a leadership role.

In our opinion, Jesse will need to work on his skating. He skates with a hunched over skating style and isn't always aware of his surroundings. It hurts his ability to make plays and he might get caught with his head down one of these times and could suffer an injury.

Forsberg is on the right track though, and is looking like a late first round pick at this time. It will be interesting to see how he progresses in his draft year on a stronger Prince George squad. Hopefully oft injured Brett Connolly will be able to take some of the heat off the youngster next season which should help as well.

Other Credits

Team or League logos used in this guide are property of the respective teams or league.

HockeyProspect.com

Founder – Mark Edwards

Scouts

Ron Berman
Rob Basso
Alex Linsky
Dave Toledano
Bruno Simard
Alessandro Seren Rosso
Mark Edwards
Dan Rogers
Tyler Neisz

And a few guys who prefer to remain nameless…

HockeyProspect.com also takes advantage of a huge network of fantastic hockey people we use worldwide. There are instances where we need extra input or information on a player. We are able to shrink the globe and call on these contacts.

We remember the late Jim Koleff for helping us build some of these relationships.

Website Writers

Alex Linsky

Andrew Echevarria

Steve Fitzsimmons

Media Relations

Steve Fitzsimmons

Stay up to date with the most recent information leading up to the NHL Draft.

Visit HockeyProspect.com for all your prospect news.

HockeyProspect.com
contact@hockeyprospect.com

1.877.473.7238

**OAKVILLE ONTARIO
CANADA**

www.ingramcontent.com/pod-product-compliance
Lightning Source LLC
LaVergne TN
LVHW051041080426
835508LV00019B/1645